AF573389

The Gloves of IRONY

The Gloves of IRONY

Rod Marsh

Pelham Books

CONTENTS

Acknowledgements

I would like to acknowledge the following who have helped with pictures, cartoons and illustrations:

PBL Marketing Cricket Library
Patrick Eagar
Ken Kelly
Bill Mitchell *(The Australian)*
Tandberg *(The Age,* Melbourne*)*
Jon *(Daily Mail,* London*)*
Birmingham Post & Mail
The Sydney Morning Herald
Sydney *Sun*
The Age (Melbourne)
The Herald & Weekly Times (Melbourne)
Press Association
Universal Pictorial Press
Garth Dawson & Co. (Accrington)

First published in Great Britain by
Pelham Books
44 Bedford Square
London WC1B 3DU
1982

First Published in Australia by
Lansdowne Press

British Library Cataloguing in Publication Data

Marsh, Rodney
Gloves of irony
1. Marsh, Rodney
2. Cricket players-Australia-Biography
I. Title
796.35'8'0924 GV915.M/

ISBN 0 7207 1443 5

Typeset by S. A. Typecentre
Printed by Tien Mah Litho Printing Co. (Pte) Ltd.,
2 Jalan Jentera, Jurong Town, Singapore.

This book was set in Century Schoolbook, 10 on 11 point.

Introduction

It is fair to say this book was born of self-defence.

Too many questions were left unanswered about Rodney Marsh after the Australian cricket team's 1981 tour of England.

Was Marsh — 'Old Irongloves' — the type of man who would punch innocent bystanders and wreck dressing-rooms?

Is he the type of man the press would have you believe?

The book was written, not to clear my name, but merely to tell my side of the stories.

It developed from there to include highlights of the 1981-82 Australian summer, and our tour of New Zealand.

I hope you enjoy reading it as much as Austin Robertson and I enjoyed writing it.

Rod Marsh

Rodney Marsh

A man called Peter

THE VERY LAST thing I needed on the afternoon of August 2, 1981 was a Pommy bloke named Peter Jennings.

To lose a Test match is one thing. To lose a Test you should have won easily is another. And when that Test means the difference between winning, drawing or losing a series — particularly an Ashes series — then that's another thing again.

The Edgbaston crowd observed our disgraceful attempt to salvage self-respect.

I don't like to lose. I have been described at various times as a "fierce competitor". And if that means hating to lose, then that's what I am.

The Fourth Test of the 1981 tour, at Edgbaston, was a total disaster for Australia. We needed only 151 runs in favourable batting conditions to take a 2-1 lead in the series, but we could scrape together only 121. On top of the humiliating defeat in the previous Test, at Leeds, it was a devastating happening.

Peter Jennings, English Test match watcher, who made a small niche for himself in Anglo-Australian cricket relations during the fourth Test at Edgbaston in 1981.

There were excuses for the Leeds defeat. The pitch heavily favoured all the pace bowlers and, of course, there was that superb 149 not out by Ian Botham in England's second innings.

You could accept Botham's innings as something of a miracle, a masterpiece in courage and swashbuckling good fortune. I'd have enjoyed it a lot more had I not watched it from behind the stumps.

The Edgbaston Test was our chance to salvage self-respect. And what did we do? We blew it. Disgracefully.

Our second-innings' target would have been considerably less than 151 but for some very ordinary bowling on our part in England's second innings. Our bowlers conned themselves into believing all they had to do to clean up the England tail was roll the arm over. Still, 151 should have been a cakewalk. We were going along fairly comfortably, too, at 3/87 — then up bobbed Botham again.

Hadn't he done enough?

You know the rest of the sorry story. Botham took 5/1 in one of

Playing into England's hands – Kim Hughes and his hook shot off Willis which brought his dismissal at Edgbaston.

the most shameful batting collapses in cricket history. I was one of Botham's victims, but somehow the magnitude of his performance didn't really sink in until after the presentations on the Edgbaston balcony.

Five for bloody one! I still couldn't believe it.

Anyone who's played cricket with me knows me as a bloke who loves to join the boys in a pot or two after a day's play. But not this time. Not this particular day. It had been the most disappointing experience of my life and, like Greta Garbo, I wanted to be alone.

I went downstairs to the dressing-room, sat in a corner and thought of what might have been. I thought about our top-order batsmen in general and about our skipper, Kim Hughes, in particular. I thought what might have happened if Hughes had not played a stupid hook shot when the Poms had two men stationed out in the deep for precisely that stroke. Christ, a captain is supposed to lead by example. What Hughes did would have been an example for a kamikaze pilot!

I thought about the way we'd all capitulated out there that day without so much as a squeak. I wondered what the hell I'd ever done to so offend the Creator.

Then I cried.

It's funny, really. I don't recall the tears welling up inside. But suddenly I was sobbing. Unashamedly, as they say in the best sellers.

I don't know how long I sat there but there were tears and a lot of bullock driver phrases. I guess it was out of sheer frustration and anger.

Here we were, down 2-1 in the series when it should have been 3-0 in our favour. The Ashes should have been safely in our keeping.

We'd had our share of bad luck with injuries. Geoff Lawson and Rodney Hogg had broken down, which put an enormous workload on Dennis Lillee, Terry Alderman and Ray Bright. I guess if Hogg had been able to bowl in England's second innings at Edgbaston, he may have been able to rip through the tailenders. We simply did not have a fresh bowler to fire at the Poms.

But we should never have lost that Fourth Test. Instead of sitting there in the dressing-room. I should have been out drinking vintage champagne like it was illegal.

Anyway, there I was on my own and listening to the mob outside, in various stages of hysteria, chanting "England . . . England . . ."

The unfortunate thing was that, having been badly beaten, we had to run the gauntlet of hundreds of England fans — most of them jeering and sneering — to reach the team bus. It was probably about 200 metres. It seemed longer.

Some were seeking autographs but most of them just wanted to give us a bad time.

"You're useless!" was one of their kinder descriptions of us.

Having reached the bus, I realised I'd left some photographs back in the dressing-room. I wanted them badly because they were pictures of the catch I'd taken in the Third Test at Headingley to give me the world wicket-keeping record. An English press photographer had given them to me and there was no way I was leaving the ground without them.

So again I ran the gauntlet. To the dressing-room and back.

Same reaction. Same abuse.

I was approaching screaming point when I got back to the bus, this time with a couple of beers — one for me, one for Martin Kent (who had put in an order).

I sat down and had just opened my can when our physiotherapist, Derek Adler, said: "Hey, have a look at this guy!"

We did — and what we saw was a bloke hanging over the top of a six-foot high fence. He was standing on the railing, which was probably a foot off the ground, and sort of draped over the top of the fence. He was shouting something we couldn't hear because sensibly, the windows were closed, but there was no doubt what his hands were saying. They were giving us the big thumbs-down.

This bloke had chosen a bad time to rubbish us because we'd been talking about the reception the mob had given us and a few of the boys had expressed the desire to punch a head or two.

I looked at this clown for maybe a few seconds. And I snapped. It had been a very bad day. I'd had enough.

I got off the bus, slipped past our manager, Fred Bennett, and walked at a fairly brisk pace towards our antagonist. As I approached, he said: "You Australians are a load of rubbish . . . you're just rubbish — you're rubbish . . . the whole lot of you."

Then he said an amazing thing: "Yes, and you're one of them, Lillee. You're a load of rubbish — you're nothing but a load of rubbish."

In favourable circumstances, I'd have got a giggle out of that. You see, there's all of 6 ft. of 'FOT' (Lillee) and only 5 ft. 8 in. of 'Bacchus'. It showed me how much he knew about cricket.

Instead of giggling, I gave him a burst that even in these permissive days, could only make the pages of this book as an asterisk.

There was no-one else within earshot, so I said a few more words, none of them complimentary. I got to the fence and made a quick jump at him — all of that 5 ft. 8 in. of me. He went off that fence faster than I thought possible and fell all of 12 inches to the ground.

"I'll sue you, Lillee," he shouted. "I'll sue you."

This is a bit of all right, I thought. I've got my mate into trouble, but I'm okay. I tried to grab him through the fence but unfortunately by now he was too far away for my short arms. And that fence was higher than me, by a considerable margin.

By this stage, Fred Bennett was on the scene.

"Righto," he said, "you get back on the bus. I'll sort this out."

My friend and I exchanged a few parting niceties, he again threatening to sue Dennis Lillee, me saying "You'll get your bloody chance to sue if you jump the fence and come over here."

And with that, I left Fred to it. The last thing I saw was Fred pointing his finger at him as he explained a few of the finer points of sportsmanship.

The miracle-worker. Ian Botham's five wickets for one run made me cry. He took all five in 28 balls.

When I got back on to the coach, our driver — a delightful Englishman, Peter Tribe — said he had the feeling it would be a good idea if he went and had a few words with the bloke. Peter, who had adopted us all, had done a bit of amateur boxing in his army and merchant marine days and seemed keen to loosen a few teeth. We talked him out of it.

As we drove out of the ground, I noticed the fence finished only about 150 yards from the point of our altercation. So my opponent had, in fact, been accessible all the time. I was quite disappointed.

I regarded the incident as finished. Other people didn't. When I left our hotel the following morning, I was besieged by reporters and television cameras. A TV guy rushed at me and asked me for a comment.

Comment? I didn't even know what he wanted me to comment about. The weather, perhaps? The loss of Edgbaston?

I set him straight anyway, reminding him that only the manager and captain were empowered to comment on anything.

I went back into the hotel and asked Fred Bennett what was going on. He told me the bloke I'd tangled with at Edgbaston was Peter Jennings, press secretary to the Bishop of Birmingham. He also said that, according to the Australian Press guys, Jennings had told his story to the newspapers and was making one hell of a fuss.

It still didn't worry me. After all, Jennings couldn't tell me from Dennis Lillee! As it turned out, he knew by this time that I was, in fact, Rodney Marsh. Jennings had phoned and apologised to Fred. And Fred said he was sorry it all happened too.

The response to the Jennings incident was amazing, both in the media and in my personal mail. The media blew it up out of all proportion. If you'd believed what you read, you'd have sworn I had been involved in the biggest stoush since World War II. In fact, not a blow was struck.

I was dammed annoyed when I learned later that back home in Perth, the evening *Daily News* had come out with a picture of me punching a football while training with the West Australian state football squad just before I left for England. I suppose the picture was the newspaper's quaint way of demonstrating my punching power. Since no punch had been thrown at Edgbaston, I thought the picture quite unnecessary and more than just a little cruel.

My mail on the Jennings row was a mixture of support and animosity. Most of the English people who wrote to me were on my side. Some of them went so far as to suggest it was a pity I hadn't actually got hold of Jennings and remodelled his facial features.

Other letters were quite abusive. One of them challenged me to a fight outside the Oval after the final Test. I didn't open this one until a couple of weeks after I returned home. I would not have accepted the challenge anyway. I'm no great pugilist and my hands are much too valuable to risk in a punch-up anyway.

The Jennings episode stayed with us right to the end of the tour. His statements kept coming — among them the accusation that Fred Bennett had been rude in not answering one of his letters. But both Fred and I had seen and heard quite enough of Mr. Peter Jennings, thank you very much.

During the Sixth Test, Jennings wanted to meet me and discuss our Edgbaston confrontation. Fred passed on the message but he and I agreed that such a get-together would be unwise because maybe it would rekindle my previous desire to whack him. So the meeting never came about. Fred spoke with him during that Oval Test and all Jennings wanted to talk about was Edgbaston. Fred short-circuited a long, over-dramatised and boring re-enactment of the incident by telling Jennings that the matter had been closed for some time and he would not discuss it with him.

The matter had indeed been closed — as far as we were concerned. But for a minor incident, precipitated by Jennings' performance on that fence, it was certainly given over-amplification by an over-zealous media with nothing better to do. I regret to have to assure Peter Jennings that the whole affair cost me not a wink of sleep.

Gentlemen (and others) of the Press

YOU MAY THINK that I am less than fond of the media, particularly in England. And you would be right. My whinge is that the press, television and radio people are altogether too eager to ignore the main issues and frantically seek out the so-called "sensational sidelights". And having sought them out, they so often get them wrong.

At Northampton in 1975, I was given out just before stumps in what I considered was a very dubious decision. I wasn't happy, but neither was I about to tear the stand down.

I walked into the pavilion to be confronted by some bloke, a Pom, who started to abuse me. He certainly wasn't a member of my fan club! My only response was to ask him, ever so politely, for his membership number. He wasn't about to oblige so I turned my back and walked away. A newspaper came out next morning with the story that I'd thrown a glass at one of the members! To this day, I don't know how or where they got hold of such a story. It was pure fiction.

We'd barely arrived in England on that 1975 tour when the papers had Jeff Thomson leading our blokes on a sort of Bacchanalian tour of the nightspots. Wine, women, song . . . you name it and, if you believed what you read, 'Thommo' and the boys had been in it. The fiction-writers had been at it again.

'Thommo' was probably the man England feared most following his devastating 1974-75 season in Australia. He'd just signed a $633,000 contract with a Brisbane radio station and maybe the press people thought they'd fit him up with an image to match his new-found opulence and his on-field ferocity.

'Thommo' hitting the nightclub circuit was simply not on. He was, in fact, one of the quietest tourists. He'd rather stay in his hotel room than join the chaps in the bar downstairs.

I'm not suggesting he was, or is, teetotal. When he decided it was time to have a drink, he never did things by halves. But to suggest that he'd been out all night drinking booze and chasing women was a load of rubbish. It was particularly annoying because, having been invented by the English press, the story was flashed back to Australia and did the rounds of the dailies there. The big danger was that the bad publicity could have seriously affected Thomson's performance on that tour. It didn't, but it might have.

Kim Hughes and Dennis Lillee fell victims of the "boozing bawdy Australian" misconception during the 1981 tour of

At least the cartoonists slugged us with a smile!

England. They were fortunate enough to be invited to the Isle of Man by Robert and Susan Sangster — and what did the London *Daily Mail* have to say about that? It had the Sangsters and their guests — "beer-swilling Australians Lillee and Hughes" — completely disrupting a show given on the Isle by Des O'Connor.

Kim and Dennis told me later that at the show, where Des had invited audience participation, they'd each had one glass of champagne.

The press is powerful, but what a pity it can't be accurate.

I made the headlines on the 1981 tour for chatting with a spectator during the Second Test at Lord's.

England had got off to a reasonable start and we looked like having quite a run chase on our hands. Certainly, the Poms didn't need the help they got from this bloke on the boundary.

If you know Lord's at all, you'll know that the ground immediately in front of the pavilion slopes up at quite an angle for the last two or three yards. The ball actually has to hit the wall to register a boundary.

I knew the rule well enough. I don't know if our spectator friend did, but he jumped the boundary rope and fielded the ball before it ran up the hill. There was no way that ball was going to make it to the boundary. Our fieldsman was within ten yards of it and gaining fast when this idiot picked it up and threw it back. The umpire had no option but to signal a four. It could have meant the difference between winning and losing a Test match.

I showed my displeasure by waving a glove at the bloke on the boundary and made a mental note to have a word with him when drinks came on to the field about ten minutes later. When the drinks arrived, I gave them a miss and wandered over to the boundary to have a yarn with the Poms' new-found helper. I told him we were not in the habit of coming into his loungeroom or his backyard and we'd be grateful if he'd return the courtesy and stay out of our domain which, at the moment, was the playing field at Lord's. I also told him that if he came on to the field again, I'd be very tempted to place my gloves firmly around his face.

I sensed immediately that this bloke didn't like me.

The game resumed and I forgot about our little chat . . . until next morning. And there I was again, all over the newspapers. The press had done it again — given the Test itself second billing and gone big for the poor, misunderstood fellow that nasty Rodney Marsh had singled out for abuse.

They'd interviewed this bloke and he'd come out smelling like roses. It didn't worry the newspapers that his stupidity could have changed the course of a Test match and an entire Ashes series. Or that if he'd done it at, say, the Melbourne Cricket Ground, he'd have been very smartly arrested. Oh, no. It came across as a battle between a folk hero and an uncouth colonial.

The Pommy cricket public are a mixture, some good, some pompous and self-opinionated and they can do no wrong as far as their press is concerned.

On the other hand, touring Australian teams can do very little right. It's been so ever since Fred Spofforth destroyed them that day at the Oval 100 years ago, and I doubt if they'll ever forgive him.

You have probably never heard of the Poison Typewriter Club. For its formation, we are indebted to Dennis Lillee, who coined the name during our 1977 tour of New Zealand. It stuck. In fact, the men at whom it was derisively aimed adopted it immediately.

Don Cameron, of the *New Zealand Herald*, and Dick Tucker, of the Sydney *Daily Telegraph*, are the only surviving members of the P.T.C., in that they are the only scribes to have covered both tours.

The club was born on the team bus between Auckland and Hamilton after the press contingent had asked if, for reasons of convenience, they could travel the 100-odd kilometres with us.

Our manager, Roger Wotton, had no objections but a lot of the players regarded it as a dangerous precedent. The team bus is like the dressing-room. What goes on in it is the players' business, the team's business. It is sacred. It is a place where we can swear as much as we like, do anything we like without upsetting anyone but our mates. And we do plenty of that. It has always been that way in my career and it should remain so.

We let off steam, have a drink or two or three, we play cassette music as loud as we like, we become bawdy, rude, crude, disgusting if you like. It is our way of letting off steam, or releasing a few pent-up emotions and hostilities. The last thing we need is an audience of over-zealous pressmen.

Dennis Lillee has always been a strong advocate of team privacy where it's due and he made it very clear that these blokes were not wanted *en voyage*. They came along anyway.

Dennis called them a "bunch of poison typewriters" for what they'd written about us and what they would probably write after the bus trip. He served it up to them like a nagging housewife for the entire trip. He held the floor all the way. No-one else got a word in. No-one else got a chance to do anything which the gentlemen of the press might have considered worth reporting.

But the poison typewriter bit had made quite an impact.

A couple of weeks later, in Christchurch, we learned that our unwanted bus guests had formed the Poison Typewriter Club. Their "uniform" was a green tie bearing a gold giraffe emblem and the letters "P.T.C." underneath.

The significance of the giraffe escaped us for quite some time. Then someone explained it. It seemed that these blokes dined together every night on tour and ordered many carafes of wine. As the evening wore on, and as more reds and whites were sunk, the word "carafe" became a little difficult to pronounce. So it became a "giraffe".

And if you think I haven't a nice word to say about the press, you're wrong.

Two nights before the Second Test in Auckland in 1982, we were formally invited to Don Cameron's home for a barbecue.

Ray Bright, Greg Chappell, Dennis Lillee, Kim Hughes and I accepted and rubbed shoulders with Don, Dick Tucker and the more recent members of the P.T.C.

It was a first-rate evening. Don, an eloquent wordsmith, is also a very fine host.

Don Cameron made a very valid point in a feature he wrote in the *New Zealand Herald* at the start of our 1982 tour. He mentioned the enormous impact of televised cricket on newspaper coverage.

Don put it this way:

> "If television had a good story then newspapers and radio charged after a better one. If television criticised some aspect of a game (remember the mullygrubber?) then as soon as possible the other media had to top the television comment. Rumour, speculation, guesswork . . . all grist to the publicity mill.
>
> "So if Chappell ran into a run of low scores he became the news of the day, the immediate impact (with never the balance to suggest that a man who had been a young god of a batsman must inevitably run into a mortal patch). Rumour, speculation, guesswork, the next story trying to top the old one . . ."

And that's how it goes. In pre-television days, the newspaper was the cricket fan's Bible. The cricket writer reported the day's events, the day's play, and that was that.

Not so now. He feels compelled to "scoop" the TV coverage, to go one better, to delve behind the scenes. And in the frantic process of going one better, he so often whips up controversy which simply does not exist.

A quote can so easily become a misquote — and I think people like Greg Chappell and Kim Hughes suffered badly on this score during the 1981-82 summer.

An example of the misquote was the follow-up to Kim's statement about the need for Australia to find a couple of young fast bowlers, even if it meant getting them off the beach, because the West Indies pacemen were bigger, younger and faster than ours. One newspaper had Windies skipper Clive Lloyd agreeing with that observation. In fact, Clive said nothing of the sort.

Now Clive is one of the easiest blokes in the world to get along with, but that misquote upset him so much that he would not talk to the Australian press for the last couple of weeks of the tour. And I don't blame him. If they can't get your quotes straight, it's better to say nothing at all.

Allan Border gave them a big miss, too. He refused a press conference after his magnificent century in the Third Test against the Windies in Adelaide because he was furious with what had been written about his opinion of the Melbourne wicket. The way he was quoted virtually had him saying he could bat on that wicket but Greg Chappell couldn't. Allan was so annoyed that at a team meeting before the Adelaide game he wanted everyone gagged — manager and captain included.

The cricket writer's stock answer is that he is merely doing his job and I've no doubt that he is under considerable pressure in the journalistic rat-race to wring the utmost out of every situation.

THE Sun

No 22,884

Telephone 20944 Letters to Box 506 GPO Sydney 2001

TUESDAY, AUGUST 4, 1981

20 cents*

CITY FINAL

$25,000 BINGO

BISHOP'S AIDE CLAIM

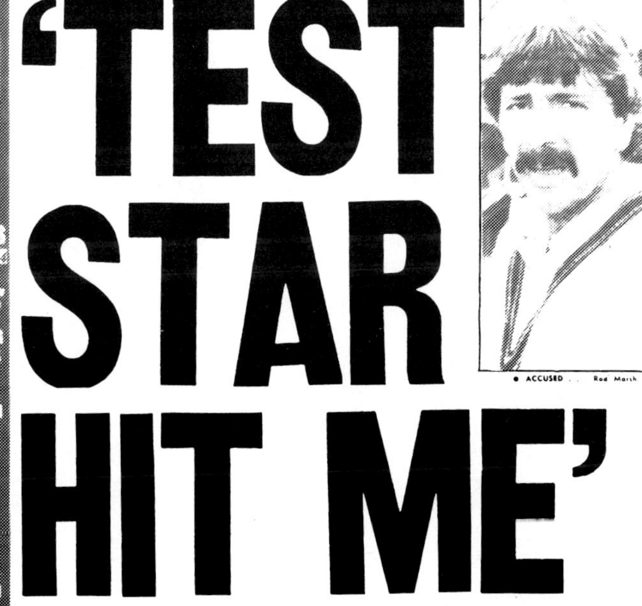

'TEST STAR HIT ME'

FASHION NEWS YOU CAN USE

TIGHTS

OFFICE GIRLS TEST THE TOP SELLERS

THEIR VERDICT: P34

DAZZLE

EXCITING IMPORTS FROM INDIA

TURN TO P36

ADAM ANT —BY HIS WIFE

SEE P14

LEAGUE

WHAT THE GREATS SAY ABOUT THE GAME TODAY: P6

● ACCUSED . . . Rod Marsh

A BISHOP'S aide has claimed he was punched and sworn at by Australian Test cricketer Rod Marsh.

"It was disgusting. I was attacked and faced a barrage of four-letter words," said Peter Jennings, press adviser to the Bishop of Birmingham.

From JENNI GILBERT in London

But Australian tour manager Fred Bennett denied any blow had been struck.

He admitted there had been "an incident — a foolish one" but Mr Jennings had behaved provocatively by giving a "thumbs down" signal to his players.

"The suggestion that Marsh threw a punch at him is just not right," said Mr Bennett.

● Continued page 2

JEFF BATE LOCKED UP OVER FINE: P3

48 PAGES TODAY | ● WEATHER: Cool. Westerly winds. (Map P32.) ● LOTTERIES: New Jackpot 1944, P41; Special 3350, P32. ● FINANCE: P41. ● TV P2?

Back in the headlines – but is it cricket?

But relations between Test cricketers and the press — in this country at least — will never improve until the newshounds skip the trivia and get on with the game.

Bloody Edgbaston

IT WOULD BE QUITE FAIR — in fact, it would be quite an understatement — to say that Edgbaston is not my favourite cricket ground. I have a lot of Edgbaston memories, and most of them are unpleasant. Quite apart from my brush there in 1981 with Peter Jennings and the streaker, there was "The Incident of the Broken Glass Door" six years earlier.

It was quite erroneously claimed on that occasion that I had, in a fit of pique, thrown a cricket bat through the dressing-room door. Now would I do a thing like that?

I was merely a victim of circumstances.

I was going along very nicely in the First Test of the 1975 tour, had reached 60-odd and was seriously thinking in terms of a century. Then the Poms complained about the state of the ball they were bowling, and the umpires agreed it was sub-standard.

The procedure in such cases is simple enough. The umpires quickly produce a substitute ball of similar condition and the game goes on. Not so that day at Edgbaston in 1975.

A suitable ball could not be found, so another — in better condition — was taken out to the nets and pounded in the turf for five minutes until it degenerated into the required state of decay. So for five bloody minutes my batting partner, Ross Edwards, and I stood out there in the middle of the ground like a couple of shags on a rock. It's the sort of stuff that does wonders for your concentration! By the time this drawn-out drama ended and play eventually resumed, I was nice and angry. And I was out very next ball. Which made me even angrier.

No-one who even vaguely fancies himself as a batsman likes to get out and it's always easy to find excuses. But I thought I had a pretty fair case this time.

Now the dressing-rooms at Edgbaston are as good as anywhere in England but while their designer knew a lot about comfort and convenience, he obviously knew next to nothing about human nature. So unfamiliar was he with the ways and temperaments of Test cricketers that he'd installed glass doors!

That wasn't smart because cricket bats are made of wood — and wood, when thrown hard enough, breaks glass. And cricketers, in moods of anger born of frustration, are apt to throw cricket bats at dressing-room doors. Hard.

However, that didn't happen in this case. Someone wiser in these matters than the architect must have started the rumour that I threw my bat through the door after leaving the field that day. Did my bat go through that door?

It is simply not true. Certainly, I thought about it. I thought

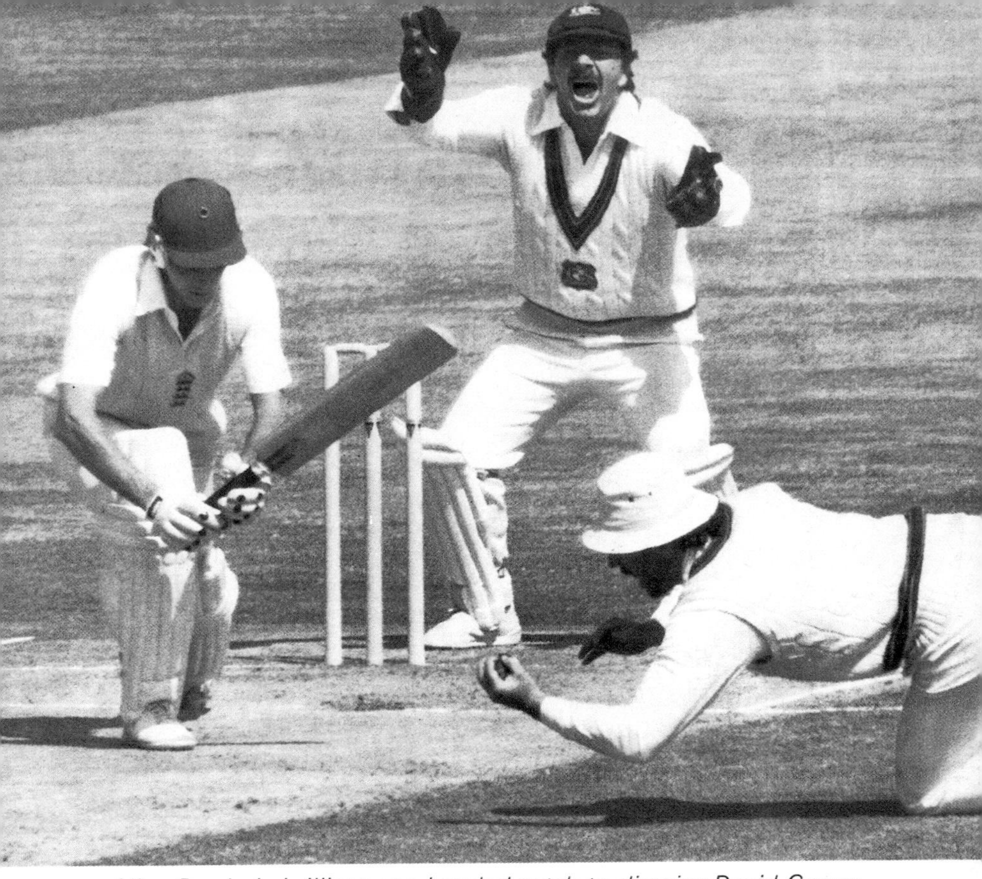

Allan Border's brilliant one-handed catch to dismiss David Gower off Bright in the Edgbaston Test match.

very seriously and decided it would be a stupid thing to do because nothing but trouble and bad publicity could follow.

Then, of course, there was the damage I may have done to my favourite bat.

No, I thought, I shall merely close the door quite firmly behind me. I did that, and nothing happened. No pent-up anger had been released. So I did it again, a wee bit harder. Nothing happened. I felt no less angry. So I did it, a third time, very hard. And the whole sheet of glass fell out.

I can recommend the sound of tinkling glass as a great soother of the savage beast. It certainly did me a lot of good.

I'm not suggesting that any cricketer, from the very junior level up, should dash about smashing doors and windows every time he loses his wicket.

But top-grade cricket is a funny thing. You're playing for your country and every time you get out, you've let your country down. It's bad enough when you're out fair and square. When you're out to a bad decision or a bad break, it can be intolerable.

Got it! I'm across in front of first slip man Graeme Wood to catch Willis off Alderman at Edgbaston.

A lot of guys can take it without showing much emotion at all. They'll sit in the dressing-room with head between hands, not prepared to show their feelings. Others — the more volatile among us — have to take it out on something.

In the Second Test of that 1975 series, I kicked a wastepaper basket several laps of the Lord's dressing-room after being given out incorrectly. The umpire ruled it a bat-pad catch off Tony Greig who was bowling spin, but there was no way the bat had been involved.

I was fuming when I got back to the dressing-room so I soccered that wastepaper basket into submission. A few of the boys suggested that I try out with Aston Villa or Manchester United. The exercise did me a lot of good. It was simply a case of releasing the anger, getting it out of the system.

I have never regarded such behaviour as bad sportsmanship; I regard it as an understandable reaction to bitter disappointment and frustration. Neither do I think these shows of anger warrant the amount of publicity they are given. They happen in

The raised fist of triumph. Botham bowls Alderman and England win, incredibly.

the dressing-room and preferably they should stay in the dressing-room, yet both these incidents found their way to the press and were treated as events of enormous significance.

The morning after the Edgbaston episode, the newspapers insisted that I'd thrown my bat through that dressing-room door. I don't know the source of their information, but it was certainly untrue.

As for the door itself, I was quite happy to pay for the damage but it never came to that.

Everyone just blamed the faulty workmanship.

The streaker who ran on to the ground during our Prudential Cup match against England at Edgbaston in 1981 caught me at a very bad moment. Bad for him, I mean.

I'd dropped two catches — both off Terry Alderman, who was

Prude

The television commentator said it was my best glovework of the day. The police who dutifully received my catch were so impressed they suggested I join the force. And I must say my catching didn't look back after the "streaker incident".

striving for a place in the First Test side — so I was in no mood to tolerate idiots.

The first chance was no sitter, but I should have gloved it. The second was probably the easiest catch I've ever put down. It just rebounded out of my gloves.

I was furious with myself for letting the team — and particularly Terry — down. I was also thinking that such a bad start to the tour could seriously damage my confidence and that it could take me a couple of Tests to get back into business. A lot of things — all depressing — were running through my mind when the streaker jumped the fence. I saw red.

For one thing, the match was at a very tight stage and the last thing anyone needed was for a guy with a load of booze aboard to appear on the field showing off what he mistakenly thinks is the body beautiful. For another, I'm anti-streaker by nature.

So I tackled this clown, brought him down and held him there until a policeman and a policewoman arrived. They laughingly suggested that I should give cricket away and join the Police Force and I agreed that at that particular time I was probably doing better at police work than at keeping wickets.

The ultimate humiliation of that day's work came when I was watching highlights of play on television that night. They showed me bringing down the streaker and Richie Benaud, doing the commentary, said: "Well, I think that's the first thing Rodney Marsh has caught all day!"

I saw the funny side and felt a lot better. What's more I started to glove the ball a lot better after that. In fact, I took five catches in the third one-day game two days later and helped us win the series.

Perhaps I should have sent the streaker a thank-you note.

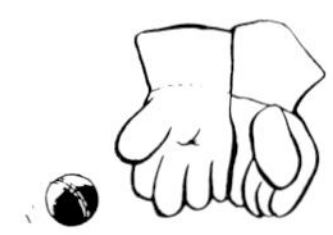

Just for the Record

BY SHEER COINCIDENCE, I passed the two big personal milestones of my career in two of the finest Test matches in cricket history.

I broke Wally Grout's Australian wicket-keeping record of 187 Test dismissals in the 1977 Centenary Test in Melbourne. It was a game which had everything and my memories of it are all the sweeter because we won.

At Leeds in 1981, I broke Alan Knott's world record of 264 dismissals in that extraordinary match which will forever be known as Ian Botham's Test. It is a game of cricket I would prefer to forget. I suppose there is some distinction in having been one of the 22 participants in that game, but I am still haunted by the humiliation of it all.

Talk about your sobering experiences!

Botham, who took us apart with his 149 not out in England's second innings, was, ironically enough, the man who had given me Knott's record in the first innings. I was well aware, when I'd caught Bob Taylor off Dennis Lillee a few overs earlier, that I had equalled Knott's record. The public-address system merely confirmed it.

Botham, so often a living example of the proposition that fortune favours the bold, had reached 50 in his own hit-a-lot-miss-a-few style and was looking very dangerous. Lillee had beaten him twice in this particular over — then he bowled him a real brute of a ball.

The wicket was hellish anyway. It was seaming all over the place and the thunderbolt Lillee sent down was perhaps as unplayable as anything I'd kept to. It pitched on or about off-stump and Botham had prematurely positioned himself to play it. The ball climbed off the pitch and flicked his glove or the shoulder of his bat, I'm not sure which.

There was a definite deflection and I took a relatively simple catch. It's the type of catch I would hope to take 100 times out of 100 — but I wasn't thinking of world records as I gloved it. I was thinking of another wicket for Australia.

Maybe the ego bit — the personal satisfaction of being the most successful wicketkeeper ever — hit me a split second later as I threw the ball into the air. I'd be less than honest if I denied feeling as tall as Joel Garner as team-mates slapped me on the back and pumped my right hand. The fact that the wicket was that of Ian Botham, off my good mate Dennis Lillee, really iced the cake.

But, truly, personal records have never been my big go. They never occurred to me when I first donned the gloves for

The record – I catch Botham off Lillee . . .

. . . and I felt as tall as Joel Garner.

Alan Knott catches Rick McCosker at Headingley, 1977. He was a class above the rest of England's 'keepers.

Australia and they have always run a distant second to my big ambitions in the game: to catch everything that comes my way, and to make maximum contribution to Australia's cricketing welfare.

Obviously, when you dedicate yourself to any facet of any sport, you strive for maximum results. If you do not, you have no right to be there. But in any team sport, the team is *the* thing and to devote yourself anything less than 100 per cent to that team is tantamount to treason.

That, at least, is the Rodney Marsh philosophy.

Comparisions in cricket don't excite me. Interest me, yes. Excite me, no. So who am I to compare my achievements with those of Knott, Bert Oldfield, Don Tallon, Wally Grout and other bygone keepers?

Certainly, I passed Knott's record in considerably fewer Test appearances. But bear in mind that I have kept very largely to great fast bowlers — Lillee, Jeff Thomson and, more recently, Terry Alderman — who seek the edge of the bat and so often find it. That is a towering advantage.

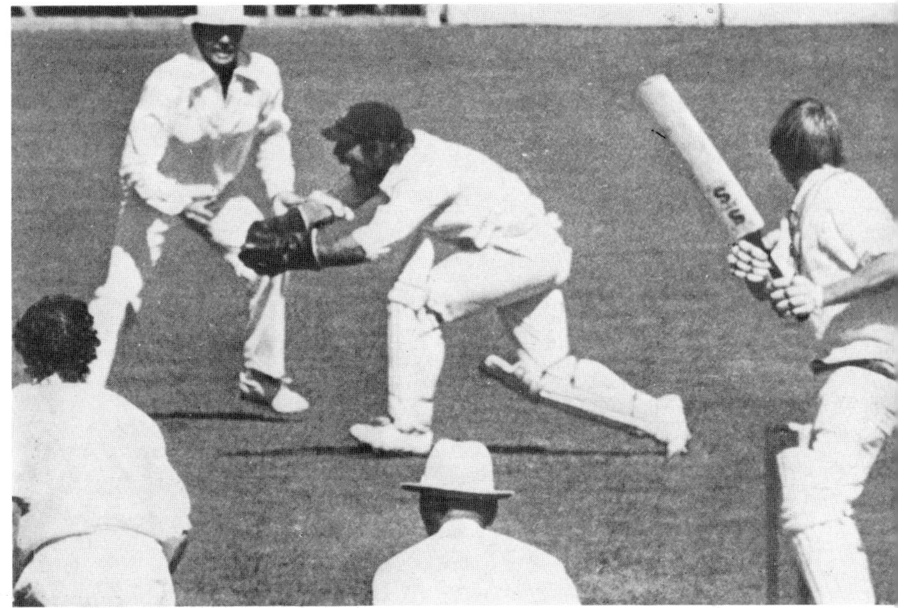

I catch England's Lever in the Centenary Test to pass Wally Grout's record . . . and unwittingly prompt a Doug Walters joke.

My "partnership" with Lillee is well-known and it is Dennis who deserves most credit. It is he, after all, who deceives the bat. I'm the "straight man" of the duo, if you like. I merely accept what comes my way. But more on that elsewhere in this book.

I was at the right place at the right time to break into the Australian Test team and, having done that, I dedicated myself to the business of staying there.

So I have two things to thank for the fact that I hold the world record — dedication, and some superb bowlers who have found the edge more than anyone else in their time.

When we arrived in England in 1981 I was, I think, 11 dismissals short of Knott's record, but I fully expected Alan to play in all six Tests. So the job of overhauling him was very much in front of me.

The England selectors surprised my by playing Paul Downton in the first Test and Taylor in the second, third and fourth before recalling Knott. They had made it so much easier for me.

I regarded Knott as a class above the rest of the England 'keepers and, if there had been a debate at the selection table, I would have expected his superior batting ability to have earned him the nod.

But who was I to complain? With Knott off the scene, I figured that, barring accident, I was going to take his world record home with me. Still, it was no big deal.

We had a tough tour ahead and the business at hand was to leave England with Ashes, not records.

The subject of my so-called pursuit of Knott's record became a bore. I couldn't be bothered discussing it with the press guys because to me it was strictly a case of first things first. The pressure from the press — and my team-mates — increased as the record loomed closer and it was a well-documented fact that when that fateful Third Test started, I was just four short of it.

Along with the elation when I took that head-high catch to dismiss Botham and break the record was a great deal of relief. Perhaps a lot of people would forget about Rodney Marsh for a while and think more about an Ashes series that was going on.

The first congratulatory phone call I received after breaking the record was from a great friend of mine, a bloke named Ian Chappell. I think the only reason he beat my wife to the phone was because the switchboard at TCN Channel 9 in Sydney was better-equipped than Telecom in Perth to get calls out of Australia.

'Chappelli' was very funny. He said: "Congratulations, pal. I'll just reiterate what Dougie said to you when you broke Wally Grout's record in the Centenary Test." I knew damn well what he was going to say, but I didn't want to deprive him of the pleasure of saying it.

"Oh yeah, and what was that, mate?" I asked.

"Well, if you'd held on to all those catches in your first Test match, you'd have passed it months ago!" he said.

Neither Doug Walters nor Ian had ever let me forget that I dropped a couple of catches in my Test debut. Remember 'Old Irongloves'?

My wife Roslyn was on the line as soon as Ian had said goodbye. They were having quite a celebration in Perth for two reasons — my record and the inevitable result of the Test (which was, of course, going to be a big win for Australia). How unkind of Ian Botham to spoil all that in the second innings. A lesser man than I might never have forgiven him for stealing my thunder.

Not long after I'd spoken with Roslyn, a parcel arrived. In it was a bottle of champagne and a note: "Congratulations. Well deserved. I hope you don't drop this one."

It was from Alan Knott. A great gesture from a true sportsman. I shall never forget it.

How long will my world record stand? Who knows?

I suppose from a selfish viewpoint, I would like it to survive until I retire, whenever that may be. It would probably give me a good deal of satisfaction to look back and think, well, I serviced my country long enough to have something to show for it.

As sure as eggs, the record will go sooner or later.

I just hope I'm still around because I'd like nothing better than to send the bloke — whoever he is — a bottle of champagne.

The magnificent Seven

SOMEONE — I think it was one of the more inspired members of the press — called us the Magnificent Seven, and it was a nice compliment. I refer to the seven West Australians among the 12 players chosen for the First Test against Pakistan in November 1981.

The statisticians have still not quite decided if so many players from one State had ever made a previous Australian Test team. Certainly not in my memory.

It would have taken the icing off the cake a little had one of us seven Sandgropers been named 12th man, but the selectors stuck to a sensible "horses for courses" policy and we were all in the playing 11. The game was, after all, in Perth — and who knows the W.A.C.A. ground better than West Australians?

It was a magnificent achievement to have seven Sheffield Shield team-mates in an Australian Test 11 and a fitting tribute to the men who had dedicated themselves, largely behind the scenes, to lifting W.A. cricket from obscurity to the top of the tree. The whole of the State was justly proud.

The surprise selection — if you could call it that — was, I suppose, Bruce Yardley. Victorian Ray Bright had, after all, been recognised as Australia's No. 1 spinner. He had enjoyed a pretty successful tour of England and had been widely tipped for a Test berth.

Bruce, however, had bowled very well against South Australia and N.S.W. at the W.A.C.A. before the Test and the selectors wisely figured that he was the man for that wicket. He justified their confidence, not only at the W.A.C.A but on every other ground as well. What a season he had. He was the real Australian success story of the summer.

Bruce is a "different" off-spinner, far more attacking than any other of his type in my experience. Perhaps at times he is too attacking and, therefore, expensive. But from a captain's viewpoint, he does a fantastic job because his natural aggression enables the skipper to put batsmen under enormous pressure. Bruce loves bowling with a lot of fieldsmen around the bat. He gets extraordinary bounce because he imparts more top spin than any other off-spinner I've seen.

He used to be a baseball pitcher and I think this has contributed a good deal to his effectiveness as a bowler. As a pitcher, he developed the "dropball" by cocking the wrist and turning the ball over top-spin fashion on delivery. He carried this style over from baseball into his days as a medium-pace bowler, then into his career as a spinner.

(From left) *Yardley, Laird, Lillee, Alderman, Wood, Marsh, Hughes.*

Bruce rarely rolls the ball out of his hand. He gives it a real flick, which probably accounts for his accuracy problem. He is a tremendously enthusiastic cricketer and if you saw any of his 38 wickets in the 1981-82 summer, you'll know what I mean. Every wicket is a personal triumph for him, and he doesn't hesitate to show his delight. His emotional victory dances are probably a legacy of the exasperating, frustrating times he had trying to win a regular spot in the West Australian team. A lesser man might well have given up in disgust and abandoned the idea of playing top cricket.

I lost count of the times Bruce swore he'd give it up. He'd have practised his heart out in preparation for a Shield match only to be told that, sorry, you're not in the team.

That would be the end for Bruce — until he slept on it and came back even more determined.

Bruce loves cricket. He loves life. He was the oldest member of our 1981-82 Test team, but he certainly didn't show it. There is a lot of cricket — and a lot of wickets — left in Bruce Yardley. In fact, I doubt if we've yet seen the best of him. Not by a long way.

The other member of the Magnificent Seven considered lucky by some to have got the selectors' nod was Bruce Laird. But if it surprised some of the armchair pundits, it certainly did not surprise his W.A. or Australian team-mates.

Bruce is only a little guy, but he is all heart and guts. He is also technically correct and, in my book, the best player of fast bowling in Australia. With the spectre of the much-feared West Indies pace battery looming large, he was a natural for one of the opening berths.

As a W.A. and Australian team-mate of long-standing, I have nothing but respect for Bruce Laird's ability and courage. People say he has never made a Test century, but let's not be too quick to forget his three tons in the World Series Supertests.

Who could forget, though, his magnificent, unbeaten 117 against the Windies in the day-night game in Sydney? It was a masterpiece of grit and character against the best pace attack in the world.

Graeme Wood was the automatic selection to open the batting with Laird. He is a class batsman and his performances at top level speak for themselves.

Perhaps the one thing Graeme must learn is to get runs in both innings of a Test match. It seems he either gets them in the first or second innings. Maybe this is coincidental but I believe Graeme is aware of this and he should make a conscious effort to make runs everytime he's out there.

The selectors' decision to pluck Bruce and Graeme from the W.A. side and install them in the Test team was fully vindicated. They gave Australia the best starts we'd had in years, both in the one-day games and the Test matches.

There could be no argument against the selection of the others who comprised the Magnificent Seven.

As vice-captain, Kim Hughes had a say in the selection anyway, but that's beside the point. He certainly had the score on the board and he played some magnificent innings at vital stages that summer, particularly his Test centuries against Pakistan in Perth and against the West Indies in Melbourne. His 84 in the second innings of the Third Test against the Windies — when he could barely walk — was another example of his undoubted class.

Dennis Lillee would manage a game in most Australian Test teams and Terry Alderman had rewritten the records during the tour of England.

Dennis bowled consistently all season and in the process, of course, became the world's greatest Test wicket-taker. He was troubled by niggling injuries, but he's resigned to putting up with those until the day he retires.

Terry started the summer brilliantly but was injured towards the end of the season and his confidence and form suffered because of it. He regained form in New Zealand and will be a mainstay of the Australian Test attack for many years.

And Rodney Marsh?

Terry Alderman – setback by injury.

Well, I had a satisfactory season with the gloves. For most of the summer I kept as well as I ever had, but I was disappointed with my batting. I was starting to hit the ball again towards the end of the Australian season but, unfortunately, the horse had already bolted.

You look back on that season and all you can do is praise the Test selectors' great wisdom in selecting seven West Australians to carry the nation's colours into battle.

The Magnificent Seven. Ah yes, it has a lovely ring to it.

It was a privilege to be one of them.

W.A.'s dominance of Australian cricket in the past decade is no coincidence. It is a result, as I have said, of sheer dedication.

Many people have been involved in the metamorphosis of cricket in the West since the bad old days when we were allowed into the Sheffield Shield only on a restricted basis and were lucky to escape one game a season without a real hiding.

But three names stand out — Barry Shepherd, John Inverarity and Tony Lock, all former State captains.

Shepherd taught us that Eastern Staters weren't invincible; Lock came from England and taught us true professionalism. And Inverarity, a great leader of young men, combined Shepherd's determination and Lock's wisdom in a tireless campaign to teach youngsters what top-level cricket is all about and what it takes to make a go of it.

From that era, particularly the Lock-Inverarity era, came Dennis Lillee and Rodney Marsh. I like to think that Dennis and I have been able to pass on to the young players something of what we ourselves were taught. Enough, perhaps, to have made a useful contribution to the continued success of cricket in our beloved home State.

Another secret of W.A.'s success has been the training methods. There is no doubt that we lead the other States on this score and have done so since the early 1970s.

Special credit here must go to State squad supervisor Daryl Foster, who did a mighty job preparing the boys physically and mentally for the job of winning — and holding — Sheffield Shields. Daryl (a former Victorian, ironically enough) became so close to the squad and so much a part of the game, that he became known as "W.A.'s 13th man". His contribution to cricket in W.A. is immeasurable.

There is no doubt that success breeds success. We were very proud of the fact, that suddenly we were winners and we were not about to become losers again. Because we were winners, we were confident, and because we were confident we were always able to win the tight decisions. So we became consistent winners — and players in a team of consistent winners invariably catch the eye of the Test selectors.

In those bad old days, a West Australian could not hope to beat, say, a New South Welshman of equal ability for a place in a Test team. He had to prove that he was considerably better.

That's the difference between winners and losers.

Things have changed — my, how they've changed — for W.A. players now. It's the Eastern Staters who have to prove themselves better than the Sandgropers — and few are able to do it.

Hence the Magnificent Seven.

Just for Kicks

DENNIS LILLEE is going to wake up one morning and say to himself: "Maybe I was wrong!" And only then will he have come to terms with himself over that celebrated kick he delivered to Pakistan captain Javed Miandad in the infamous Perth Test late in 1981.

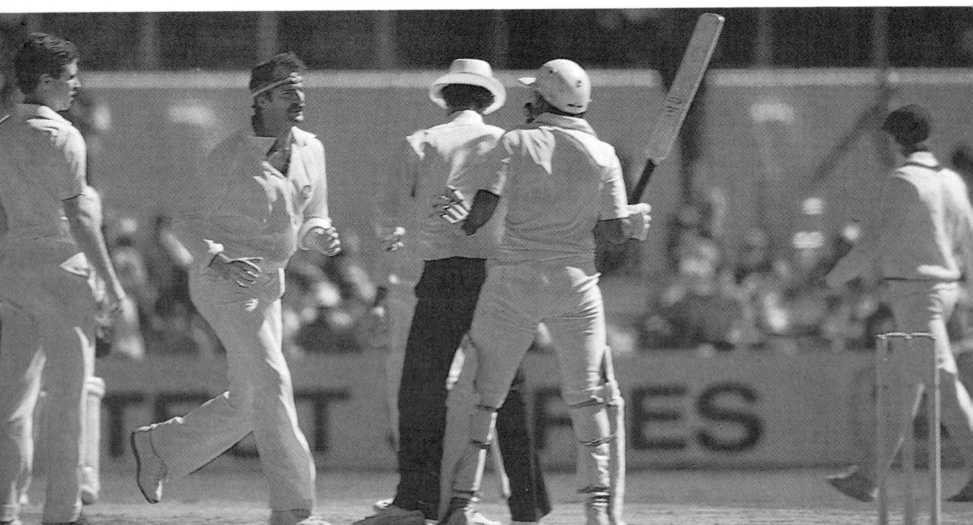

Lillee and Miandad at the W.A.C.A. ground, 1981. It was an unpleasant incident triggered by Lillee . . .

There's no doubt in my mind that Dennis precipitated the whole unpleasant affair. I've told him so several times, but he won't have a bar of it. Don't get me wrong. I'm no great admirer of Javed, other than for his cricket ability of which he has a considerable amount.

On the other hand, Dennis and I have been close mates ever since we started playing cricket together — and that goes back a heap of years. It would be easy for me to say to him: "Yeah, pal, you got a raw deal".

I think that underneath it all, Dennis believes he did wrong in kicking the little Paki. What he won't admit is that he instigated the incident.

I was there when it happened and, like everyone else, I've seen the TV replay many times. And I still can't condone anything Dennis did.

His version is that Javed poked him in the ribs with the bat as they gently collided. And I'll go along with that.

. . . still, Melbourne Age *cartoonist Ron Tandberg managed to raise a laugh.*

But in this case, the punishment didn't fit the crime. It far exceeded the crime. A dig in the ribs with a bat is not going to hurt Dennis Lillee. He's a very strong man and the only thing it would have hurt was his pride.

I think Dennis knew exactly where Javed was as the Pakistani sauntered through on that fateful run and Javed knew exactly where Dennis was. And neither was going to "lose face" by giving way no matter what the road rules are.

Certainly, had Javed veered slightly left or right, the whole thing would have been avoided. Dennis has a point there, but that's hardly the point now.

Dennis still likes to believe that Javed detonated the chain of events by lifting the bat. My interpretation is that the crunch came when Dennis threw back his hand — and missed — as Javed brushed him.

Had Dennis made contact — on the elbow, shoulder . . . anywhere — I'm sure he'd have regarded it as a one-all draw and

More fun, this time from the outer.

left it at that. You know, he hit me first, I hit him back. We're even. But having missed his mark, Dennis felt he'd been cheated. He owed Javed one.

He appealed to the umpire, complaining that Javed had hit him, but it was obvious that nothing was going to be done. So Dennis took the law into his own hands.

It was unfortunate that he kicked him. Kicking is not nice. A very gentle little kick it was, but a kick within the strict meaning of the word, nevertheless.

Clearly, the intention was to insult Javed rather than hurt him. I mean, if the object was to hurt, the kick would have been a lot harder and aimed at a different part of the anatomy.

God knows, there have been times when I'd have cheerfully taken to Javed myself because he's such an annoying little bloke.

We found it difficult to get along with him at all and the fact that most of his team-mates refused to play under him again rather indicates we were not alone in that problem area. It's not often in cricket that publicly a captain is sacked by his team and then resigns.

There is no doubt that Javed is a fine batsman but he is a little smartarse as well. Nobody, except a mother or wife, loves a smartarse, do they?

One of the reasons he's so annoying on the field is his cheek. He's a great runner between wickets and he's forever taunting the fieldsman to have a shy at the stumps. You'll never run him out, though, because he's too bloody quick, too bloody cunning. And the more he upsets you, the better player he becomes. He stokes up his batteries on upsetting the opposition.

He's the sort of bloke who particularly annoys a fierce, red-blooded, straight-ahead competitor like my mate Dennis Lillee. So I sympathise with Dennis and other bowlers, but

there's no way I'll ever say he did the right thing that day at the W.A.C.A. He was, in fact, very lucky to get off so lightly.

Chappell assisted in the first instance by putting a bit of a time fuse on the bomb that would inevitably explode by announcing after watching the replays that Javed should apologise.

The team, collectively as a Players' Tribunal, fined him only $200. It was a small monetary penalty and, I suppose, the outraged critics who said it was like being thrashed with a feather or flogged with a limp lettuce leaf, had a point.

There was no doubt the umpires, Tony Crafter and Mel Johnson, would appeal against the leniency of the penalty but I suppose they were always likely to appeal anyway, no matter what the players meted out.

I was happy with the team's decision to only fine him $200. I figured that the lesser the penalty he copped from the team, the more chance he had of getting off lightly when Bob Merriman, co-ordinator of the A.C.B.'s cricket committee, sat as a one-man tribunal to hear the umpires' appeal.

Had the team fined him heavily, it would have been a damning indictment that we regarded Dennis as very guilty and very naughty. It would have left Merriman no alternative but to hand down a more severe penalty than suspension for two one-day matches.

Perhaps Dennis deserved heavier punishment. A lot of people

thought so. The eccentrics even suggested that he be rubbed out for life, which was absurd.

Perhaps, too, the team made a bit of a mockery of the Players' Tribunal concept by fining him only $200. But that's human nature, isn't it?

We certainly didn't want Dennis rubbed out at all, but if he had to go, the two one-day B. and H. W.S.C. matches were the best ones for him to miss as far as the team was concerned.

The incident was submerged quickly in the excitement of the Tests and the Cup matches and Dennis was a very good boy after the Javed dust-up. His public apology was sensible and was just what he should have done.

Any suggestions that the incident had tarnished his hero image were erased when he at last broke Lance Gibbs' record for Test wickets. He was No. 1 boy with Australian cricket fans, no question.

Anyway, should one misdemeanour, distasteful though it may be, permanently dent the status of a man who has been such a great ambassador for Australia and Australian sport?

He has bowled longer, faster, harder and more successfully than any man in the history of the game and if he has upset a few people along the way, then that's tough.

It would be nice if a lot of other people — including those of the media and those who sit in judgement of him around the world — made as few mistakes.

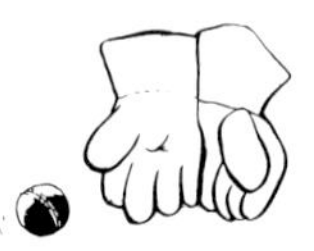

Judges and Juries

THE PLAYERS' TRIBUNAL and Code of Behaviour is an innovation which may or may not stand the test of time. The system has obvious shortcomings, as the Lillee-Javed case demonstrated.

One of my first experiences of the Tribunal was early in the summer of 1981-82 when, as a member of the W.A. Sheffield Shield team, I sat in judgement on one of my favourite people — Len Pascoe.

Lennie is a character in every sense of the word. He has a heart three times the size of his mouth and an unconscious sense of humour you wouldn't believe.

Len Pascoe was not in his most affectionate mood on the afternoon of Saturday, October 31, during the W.A.-N.S.W. Shield game at the W.A.C.A.

By his own admission, Lennie wasn't very fit. He'd had surgery on both knees during the off-season and, being the dedicated cricketer he is, was trying too hard to get fit again and impress the national selectors. It was early in the season and he should have been phasing himself in. Instead, he was punishing himself. By trying to take the strain off his still-tender knees, he was putting unwarranted pressure on his ribs and groin.

So you can see he was registering something less than 100 per cent on the fitness scale that day. Actually, it was a bit of a medical miracle that he was able to bowl at all.

Any fast bowler will tell you that when you're not fit, you don't bowl all that well. And Lennie certainly wasn't bowling all that well that day in Perth. To add insult to his considerable list of injuries, he was bowling to W.A. skipper Kim Hughes, who was in full cry and batting with the flair that only he and a few others of my experience can produce.

Kim was hitting the ball to all parts of the field and making it look so easy. And Lennie wasn't enjoying it a bit. He lost control when Kim hit one of his short-pitched deliveries over mid-wicket for four. It was a beautiful stroke but it wouldn't have hurt nearly as much if, as Lennie claimed, Kim hadn't laughed at him as he played it.

I guess there is a very thin line between a sneer and a laugh. Or between a laugh and a self-satisfied grin. (Or between that and a friendly smile.)

Lennie insisted it was, at the very kindest, a laugh.

But we must give Kim the benefit of the doubt. We won't say he laughed at Lennie; we'll say he smiled at Lennie.

Kim was obviously delighted with the way he'd played the

shot and sort of looked Lennie in the eye with a grin — or a smile — on his face.

Now that's not the sort of thing to do to Len, particularly if he's fit, because he'll just run in and bowl you another bouncer. If he's unfit, it probably is the thing to do because he'll run in and bowl you another bouncer anyway.

The difference is, of course, that a fit Pascoe bouncer is a fearsome thing and an unfit Pascoe bouncer is likely to pop up and beg to be despatched to the boundary.

But full credit here to Lennie. He took stock of the situation

The Kim Hughes-Lennie Pascoe incident – a comment from The Australian's *cartoonist, Bill Mitchell.*

and realised that if, in his jaded condition, he pitched the next ball short, it would probably rattle the pickets just as hard as the previous delivery.

No way would he fall for that. Fit, he'd have let another short one go. Unfit, he went to the other extreme and bowled the "ultimate full-toss" — the hand-to-head, or bean, ball.

There is no place in cricket for this delivery and unless the batsman is convinced that it slipped out of the bowler's hand, he is quite entitled to get uptight, very uptight. At least uptight. Possibly physical.

It is a case where strong words are the best the bowler can hope for. The worst he can expect is, I suppose, to be crowned with a cricket bat.

Having survived the bean ball, Kim marched down the wicket and told Lennie a few surprising things about himself. The atmosphere over the wicket area turned slightly blue and the scene belied the old myth about cricket being a gentlemen's game.

I thought the umpires, Don Weser and Peter McConnell, handled the situation quite superbly. So well that the game went on with minimum time lost.

Kim was out in the last over before tea so the adjournment was taken a couple of balls early. I was next man in, but with tea upon us, I took off the pads and was out back doing what we chaps do in the equivalent of the ladies' powder room when the players came of the field.

I could hear voices and I returned to the dressing-room to find an A-grade blue in progress. There was Lennie, an uninvited guest, giving Kim a nice old verbal spray. I can't recall the exact words, but they were things Miss Fiona Lilywhite never taught us at Sunday School.

Lennie's parting shot was to invite Kim outside (presumably behind the stand) to settle their differences there and then.

Kim's no fool, so he wasn't about to take on an angry Len Pascoe. I'm a sensible chap but even in my most irrational moments, I'd run a mile before trading blows with him.

I suspect the Incredible Hulk might think twice. Lennie Pascoe is one of the strongest men I've ever seen.

I'm still not sure if he was dinkum about wanting a punch-up with Kim or whether the 99 per cent hot air in him had surfaced.

I'm sure he would never have hit Kim and I'm bloody sure Kim wouldn't have hit Lennie. It would have been the greatest mismatch since David and Goliath and the result would have been far more realistic, if you get what I mean.

So Lennie left and, being a very close-knit lot over in the West, we had to do something about him.

We reported him and then the N.S.W. team, sitting in judgement on their own, suspended him for one match. You might find that hard to reconcile with the subsequent Lillee-Javed confrontation and the outcome of it. But everything, they say, is relative.

For one thing, a bean ball is a damn sight more dangerous than a gentle kick on the pad. But that doesn't really matter. It boils down to what you do on the field and off it.

Do your thing on the field, in the heat of battle, and you may get away with it. Carry it off the field and there are no such things as extenuating circumstances.

A lot of players have bowled the bean ball and escaped with nothing worse than bad publicity. But to front the offended batsman in his own dressing-room later and abuse him is a little excessive. Even the N.S.W. "Tribunal" thought so.

So Lennie copped a game's suspension, which was rather like sentencing Brer Rabbit to be thrown into the briar bush or an alcoholic to be tossed into a vat of beer.

Lennie had broken down anyway a few minutes before tea and a couple of weeks' rest was not only compulsory but desirable and absolutely necessary. If he'd been eligible for the next game he'd have played it in a wheelchair.

I don't know how he kept a straight face as the sentence was handed down.

But that's Lennie Pascoe.

Australian Test players figured in two behaviour "dramas" which eluded the eager eyes and ears of the press during the 1981-82 season.

One shall be nameless; the other is our old friend Lennie Pascoe.

The anonymous bloke incurred the displeasure and discipline of his team-mates for a remarkably vocal performance on a flight from Sydney to Perth.

We'd just lost a one-day game against Pakistan, endangering our prospects of making the series finals. It was a Thursday game and our next encounter was with the West Indies at the W.A.C.A ground on the Sunday.

The boys were pretty upset by the defeat and a little drink seemed in order. Someone produced a bottle of overproof rum in the dressing-room and the braver souls among us gave it a try. This stuff would have started a tractor. It may well have launched a rocket. Christ, was it potent!

By the time we got to Sydney Airport, several of the lads were pretty steamed up. A few more drinks in the airport bar, a few more on the plane and one of us was up, up and away. I reckon he could have flown to Perth without a plane.

It's amazing how you imagine yourself to be invisible and inaudible after you've had a few too many. This bloke certainly did, but the 180 other passengers heard every word.

The more we tried to quieten him, the louder and more outspoken he became. It became so embarrassing that the other players, through the manager, had to report him and duly fine him $300.

This particular bloke had never looked like playing up before and he's never looked like doing it since. But overproof rum can do amazing things.

I guess he just snapped. I've done it myself under pressure. I've seen plenty of others do it.

When I go haywire — maybe for a couple of hours when the pressure of cricket catches up with me — I make sure I'm locked up in the room on my own or with a few of the other players. As professional cricketers and ambassadors for our country, we cannot afford our ugly moments to go on show.

The offender on this occasion was quite happy to pay his fine when we told him what he'd been saying on the plane. The same bloke is just dying for someone else to put a foot wrong in public. He'll be the first cab off the rank with a report.

The Pascoe incident arose on the last day of the Adelaide Test against the West Indies. I like to think I nipped it in the bud and maybe saved Lennie from a last-minute sacking from the team to tour New Zealand.

I was packing my bags ready to fly home when our manager, John Edwards, told me Lennie had been reported and that the report would be phoned through to the Australian Cricket Board. As acting captain, I was bloody annoyed that I hadn't been told earlier.

I stormed into the South Australian executive room to find Colin Egar on the phone to A.C.B. Executive Director, David Richards. Egar was filing the report and saying that the umpires were sick and tired of Lennie's behaviour on the field.

Here, I thought, was a severe case of over-reaction.

Anyone — umpires included — who has been on the field with Pascoe for any length of time knows that he's full of hot air and does more talking to himself than to anyone else. Sure, he talks a lot, but that only helps to make him the character he is.

Batsmen have long since learned to ignore him. I couldn't see why umpires should take exception to him.

In this case, his "crime" had been to tell umpire Robin Bailhache it was time for him to retire. Apparently it hurt Robin's feelings and he complained to Egar. It was probably fortunate for Lennie that I walked into that room as Egar was filing the report and not after he'd done it. As it was, I was able to do a little fast talking on Lennie's behalf.

I spoke with Richards and assured him and Egar that I would talk to Pascoe and tell him how close he'd gone to being left out of the team for New Zealand. The team hadn't been announced at that stage but I knew he was in it.

Cool heads prevailed. Richards phoned Pascoe next morning

Lennie Pascoe and the man he wanted to retire, umpire Robin Bailhache.

and the matter was settled amicably and without publicity. I'm damned glad it never made the papers because it had been such a good Test match. The last thing we wanted to read about was an Australian player being reported.

Lennie Pascoe was the innocent bystander to another behaviour incident that summer — and he got quite a giggle out of it.

Pascoe had already been suspended for his brush with Kim Hughes in Perth, and Dennis Lillee for the celebrated Javed Miandad kicking affair.

Lennie was looking around for the next victim and he decided it would be new South Australian Shield captain David Hookes. He mentioned it to David before the S.A.-N.S.W. match in Sydney in December.

"Well, David", he said, "it's for sure and certain that you'll be the third leg of the trifecta. I've looked around at all the other players and you're the only one liable to get suspended!"

David was horrified that such a thing would even be suggested.

"Heavens no," he said, "I'm a changed man. I'm a captain now. You won't hear me swearing too often and you certainly won't hear me disputing decisions. I'm a changed man."

Only a few days later, David was on the mat for kicking over the stumps and accusing the umpires of poor sportsmanship after rain had robbed South Australia of certain outright victory.

The South Aussies needed only 11 runs when the umpires decided the weather was unfit for play to continue. David insisted the rain was light; John Dyson and Rick McCosker said it was heavy. Who do you believe?

Anyway, Pascoe dipped out on his big trifecta. David was fined — a full match pay — not suspended.

The South Australian skipper had last laugh, though, by leading his team to an astonishing Shield success.

Obviously, he has the makings of an outstanding captain.

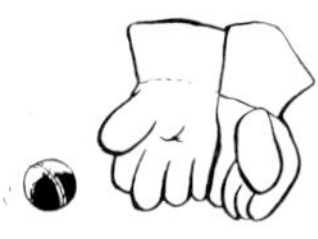

Number One

I FIRST RAN ACROSS this kid when we were both playing grade cricket in Perth.

He was tall, lean and angular. He wore long side-leavers, which were all the rage at that time. He had a very skinny face and a rather prominent nose.

He looked a bit like a hawk.

I saw him bowl from a very long run-up and with an action which was far from perfect.

Occasionally, he'd get it right and the ball would swing away from the right-handed batsman. But mostly he'd "fall over" and the ball would disappear down the leg side.

He was usually short, but always quick. The impression he left wasn't exactly indelible. He was certainly not going to set the world afire.

His name was Dennis Lillee.

I didn't think much of — or about — this guy until we played for the W.A. Colts against S.A. in Adelaide in 1967. He'd improved some since I last saw him and he impressed me a bit. But not as much as another team-mate, a fast-medium pacer named Stan Wilson.

Dennis eventually got the nod ahead of Stan for the Sheffield Shield team because he had genuine pace.

He made his W.A. Shield debut in 1968 — and the man who would be king was born. So was a great and lasting mateship between Dennis Lillee and Rodney Marsh.

Dennis is perhaps the greatest fast bowler the world has seen. A lot of people say so. The records say so. I'm not prepared to go quite that far because I believe it is impossible to compare eras. There are too many intangibles.

But he is the greatest fast bowler I have ever seen.

The statistics speak for themselves. More Test wickets than any other bowler and no telling how many more before he does Australian cricket a great disservice by deciding to retire some day.

Five or more Test wickets in an innings 22 times; 10 or more wickets in a match seven times; he has been Man of a Test series twice, won several Man of a Test match awards (it should have been one more — remember how they overlooked him in the Centenary Test Match played in Australia, giving the award to Derek Randall?).

He has turned the tide of more games than anyone — friend or foe — in my experience.

But statistics don't even scratch the surface of the Dennis Lillee story. What of Dennis Lillee the man of courage, the inspiration? What of his unmatchable ability, both on and off the field, to motivate players around him?

His desire to succeed — be it for his club, his State or his country — is infectious. He is a winner, and it rubs off on those he is among.

Dennis has given journalists more to write about than any other cricketer. He has become a superman to his team-mates, his opponents and the public.

A measure of Dennis Lillee the man is his relationship with autograph hunters. I don't believe he's ever said no. If he had a dollar for every autograph he's signed, he'd be matching millions with the Saudi Arabian oil sheiks.

Autograph-seekers can be the source of considerable annoyance to a professional cricketer. Sure, it's no big deal, no ordeal, to sign your name. But when you're besieged by a couple of hundred fans thrusting books into your face, it can wear the patience thin.

Not so Dennis. He has always regarded the autograph hunters as an important part of the cricket scene. He'll sign his name anywhere, on anything, any number of times.

And don't the kids respond to him! Ask them their favourite cricketer and if they don't say Dennis Lillee, they're not being fair dinkum.

Dennis Lillee today is a far cry from the guy we knew in the late 1960s and early '70s. When he started playing first-class cricket, he was the most gullible person I'd met. He'd believe anything!

I was on my way to the Gabba ground in Brisbane during a Shield match against Queensland in 1968-69 when the taxi-driver told me there would be a violent storm that afternoon. Cab drivers know about this sort of stuff. I asked him what time it would happen and he said: "Oh, about 3.15."

Being pretty young and gullible myself those days, I assured my team-mates when I got to the ground that there would be an electrical storm at precisely 3.15. They thought I'd gone troppo.

Whether it was extraordinary luck, or whether that cab driver was a meteorological genius, I don't know. But at 3.15 — right on the button — down it came. And if you've ever seen it rain in Brisbane you'll agree that it really rains.

We had two or three inches in a helluva hurry and the ground was awash. Next day, the *Courier-Mail* came out with a "trick" photograph of an empty beer can floating in front of the sightscreen at the Stanley Street end of the ground. The photographer had used a wide-angle lens and a lot of initiative and had brought the beer can up to look about the size of a 44 gallon drum.

I was rooming that trip with Derek Chadwick, who couldn't

The young Lillee – "quick", even then.

resist the temptation of having a little fun at young Lillee's expense.

We woke Dennis and Derek said: "Christ, did you see the picture in today's paper! There's a 44 gallon drum floating across the Gabba — how deep must the water have been out there??"

Dennis looked at the picture and said: "Gee, I knew it rained, but I didn't think it rained that much!"

Yes, Dennis was a pushover for a practical joke in those days.

Actually, he never forgot that beer can episode. Even these days, when it rains at the Gabba, he'll look at me and say: "You bastard — there'll be no bloody 44 gallon drum floating out there tomorrow!"

As gullible as he was early in his career, there was also a lot of brashness about the guy.

Dennis took five wickets in the first innings of his first Test — against England in Adelaide in the 1970-71 season — and it wasn't his fault that we were left with an enormous target for victory. We had five sessions in which to score the runs and it was never really going to be on.

Still, Bill Lawry and Keith Stackpole, who opened the innings, weren't about to surrender without a fight and were still together at tea. As they walked into the dressing-room, Dennis looked them square in the eye and said: "Keep it up, youse blokes — you're doin' real suave!"

It was hardly the sort of thing for a young bloke playing his first Test to say to a couple of old campaigners like 'The Phantom' and 'Stacky' — but then Dennis Lillee was no ordinary bloke.

There, was, of course, his well-documented meeting with the Queen at Buckingham Palace in 1972.

"G'day," said Dennis to Her Majesty.

Suppose it had been an audience with the Pope? Chances are Dennis would still have said "g'day".

The Dennis Lillee way has always been straight ahead. He says exactly what he thinks. It has won him a lot of friends and fans. It has won him a few of the other variety, too. But that's their misfortune.

The big difference between the Lillee we knew and the Lillee we know is that far from being the butt of a joke, now he is ruler of the roost.

He learned very quickly. Far from being the victim of the practical jokes, he's the bloke who perpetrates them. He's the man with the wisecrack — and everyone listens.

A trick photo and Lillee still recalls the day his team mates "gave him the drum".

W. AUST
QLD
BOWLERS
BATTING
BATSMEN
SUNDRIES
UMPIRES
ROWAN
ENRIGHT
FLY
QANTAS
TO THE WORLD
ROTHMANS THE GREAT
ASL

He's the man who can't be fooled because he's always one step ahead.

He's on top of the heap and he has earned the privilege.

Dennis Lillee really came of age as a Test bowler on the 1972 tour of England. Despite gnawing symptoms of the back injury which was to threaten his career, he bowled faster than at any other time in my experience of him.

Maybe the slower English wickets drove him to strive for that extra yard of pace. Perhaps, in retrospect, he overdid it and aggravated the injury.

He showed his maturity by bowling a much better line, too. He had always gone flat-out for maximum pace — he knew no other way — but now he could control direction and length as well.

From the very start of that tour, he was under an injury cloud and in doubt for the Tests. He played in all five, however and took 31 wickets for the series.

Gee, he was quick, but never quicker than one memorable day on a slow wicket at Leicester. It was shortly after the Lord's Test in which Bob Massie took those 16 wickets. Perhaps it would have been fairer if Bob and Dennis had taken 10 each because they both bowled magnificently.

Anyway, Dennis got very angry during the Leicester game. I think the umpire brought it on by giving Roger Tolchard not out when Dennis believed he'd had him caught at short-leg. I caught Tolchard off Dennis' next delivery, but he was still damned annoyed and proceeded to produce the fastest spell of bowling I've seen from him. Or from anyone else, for that matter.

This was Dennis Lillee at his blistering best. The ball positively hurt as it thudded into my gloves. But it was a lovely feeling.

He was in similar form during the Fifth Test at the Oval. One particular delivery sticks in the mind — the ball that got Alan Knott in the second innings.

Knotty was always a blighter to dislodge from the crease, particularly when he'd got his eye in. He certainly had it in that day. He'd been there for two or three hours — yet Dennis beat him with sheer speed and clean-bowled him. Alan acknowledged the ball for what it was — a bloody ripper.

Dennis won a very vocal fan during that Oval Test, a huge West Indian gent with whom we later got to have a few beers. Built like Muhammad Ali, he was, and with a booming voice to match his size. Every time Dennis was spelled during that Test, our friend would bellow to skipper Ian Chappell: "Mr. Chappell, let The Tiger loose. We want to see The Tiger bowl!"

Every time Dennis was tossed the ball for another bowling stint, this guy would go off his face, leaping, shouting and thanking Chappelli for his generosity and wisdom.

Dennis didn't let him down, either. He bowled superbly.

The 1972-73 season in Australia against Pakistan started very well for Dennis. He looked like doing anything, but then that back started to act up again.

It really started to go during the Third Test of that series, in Sydney. I believe Dennis knew it was something quite serious, but he is a real fighter.

To ease the pressure and pain he bowled at a slightly reduced pace, for probably the first time in his career. He did it very well, too, tying down one end while Max Walker mesmerised the batsmen at the other end. Max took 6/15 — an incredible, match-winning performance when all had seemed lost.

I think Dennis was more or less living in hope when we left on the West Indies tour in January, 1973. Underneath, he was a very worried man. The pain in his back was getting worse all the time.

He played in a couple of the warm-up games and bowled on a restricted basis in the First Test. He didn't bowl again on that tour. It was doubtful if he would ever bowl again.

When Dennis returned to Perth, the injury was diagnosed as stress fractures of the back. That's about the worst thing that can happen to a fast bowler.

It would have been very easy for him to say there and then: "Well, that's it — I've had enough."

He'd always believed he wasn't going to be playing top-level cricket for too long because he loved his home life so much. He still does. But I think the excitement — the glamour, if you like — of the international cricketer's life had got the better of him.

So Dennis decided he'd give it a go. He'd try to beat that back injury. If he failed, he'd be no worse off anyway. And if he succeeded, maybe — just maybe — he'd force his way back into the Australian Test team.

He worked like a man possessed, and it's impossible to say enough about the man who guided and nursed him along the comeback trail. I refer, of course, to Dr. Frank Pyke.

Dr. Pyke dedicated himself to the physical rehabilitation of Dennis Lillee. He put a plaster cast on the injured back for six weeks; he had him in braces and all sorts of gear. He mapped out a scientific programme of exercises and therapy. Dennis wasn't allowed to fart without Frank Pyke knowing about it.

Dennis had declared 1973-74 a season of total rest from first-class cricket, but a guy like that can't stay out of the game completely. He captained his club side, Perth, in the grade competition that season — as a batsman. And he did very well, knocking up 600 runs.

Towards the end of the season, he was bowling again — from a short run — and taking wickets. He was largely responsible for

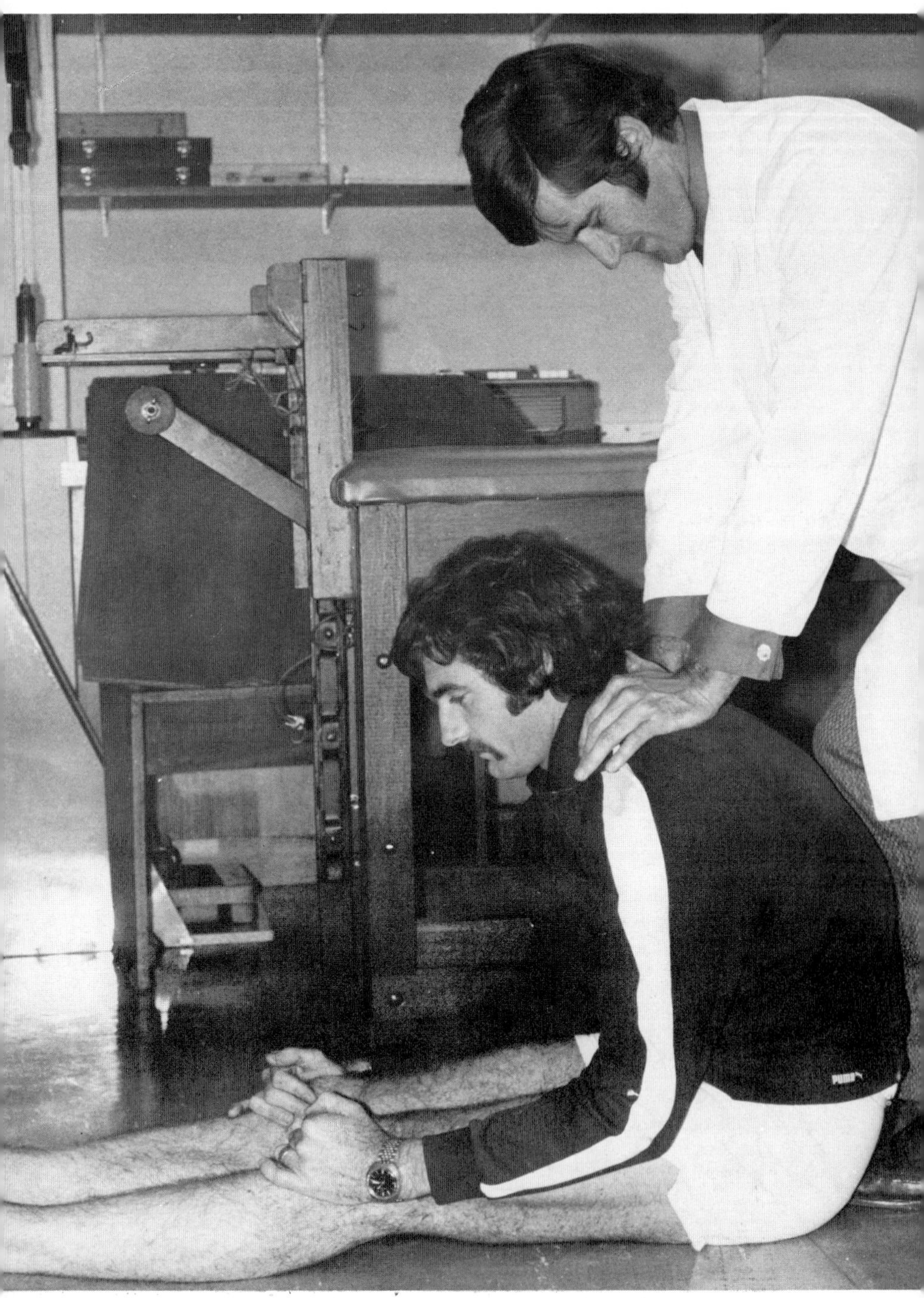

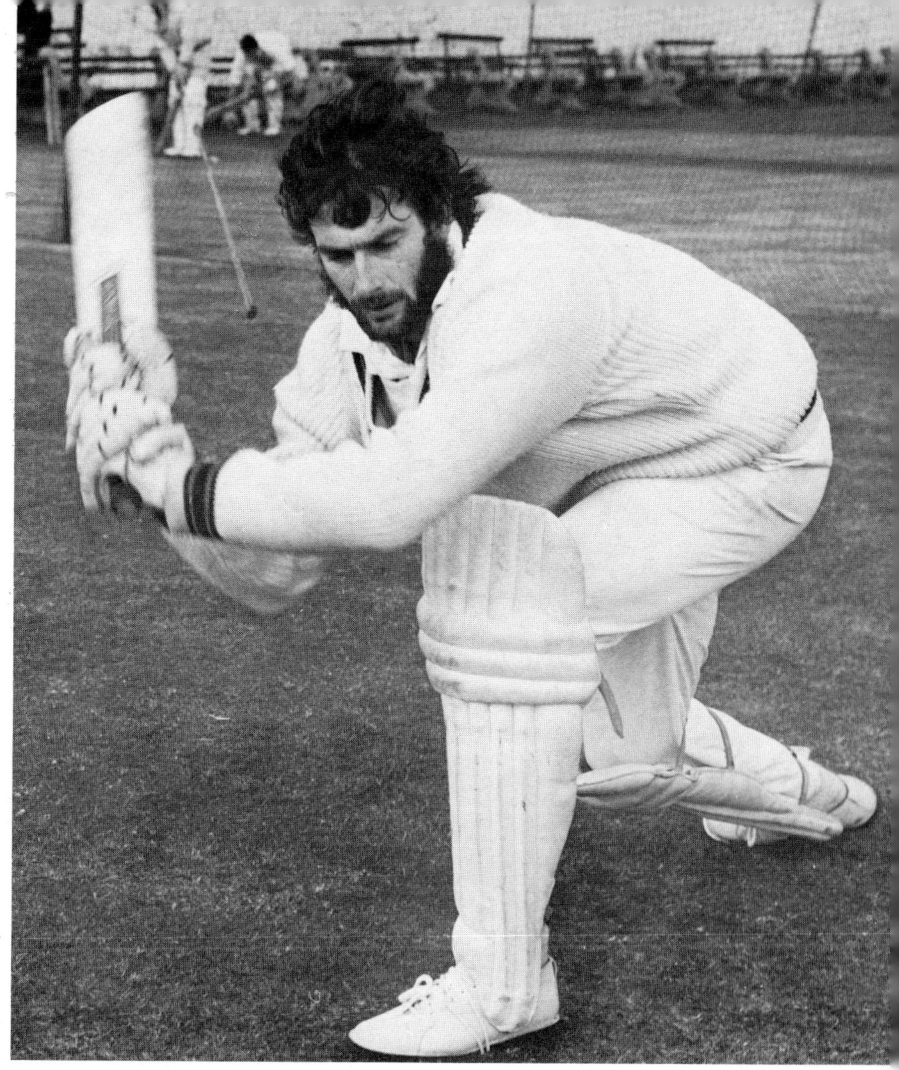

(Facing page) *Lillee on the way back with a helping hand from Dr Frank Pyke.* (Above) *Lillee's determination, evidenced by his batting success during injury.*

Perth making the final (which they lost).

If he had already worked hard to mend that crippled back, he applied himself even more so in the winter of 1974. The incentive was the upcoming tour by the Englishmen and the prospect of regaining the Ashes.

By the first Sheffield Shield match of 1974-75, he was raring to go but probably not really ready, psychologically at least.

Lillee's recovery was going to be the biggest individual story of the summer and the press were driving him nuts. He had interviews, he had advertising contracts — he had everything coming at him at once.

It reached the stage where, to his great credit, he said to hell with everything else, all I want to do is bowl.

You could see him improve game by game. He knew he'd never be able to bowl as fast as he had before the injury, but by the end of the series he had regained considerable pace. As his back continued to withstand the increasing strain he was putting on it, so his confidence improved.

He continued to follow the Frank Pyke programme and he began to realise that far from straining his back, bowling was actually strengthening it.

Dennis didn't get a great bag of wickets that summer. He didn't have to — Jeff Thomson got enough for everyone. Certainly enough to win back the Ashes.

But personal wickets were secondary to Dennis in the long term. The big thing was that Dennis Lillee had passed the big Test. He was back in business — and that meant Australia was back in business as well.

Those stress fractures actually did Dennis and Australia a favour.

Before they sidelined him, Dennis' attack was based on speed, speed and more speed.

When the injury forced him to slow down, he was smart enough to realise that he would have to develop something else — let's call it cunning — to supplement the pace he had left.

He experiemented, and God only knows how many hours he put into it. But the results were quite exceptional. He developed a lethal, three-pronged armoury:

- There is his pace, which is still frightening enough — and still quite good enough to produce the superb outswinger with the new or newish ball.
- Then there is a very quick medium-pacer, from the shorter run, which produces the real seamer.
- And there is the ability, also from the shorter run, to roll the fingers across the ball and bowl the magnificent leg-cutter.

The change of style, the new approach, wasn't an immediate sensation. But Dennis kept working on it — and you know the rest. It is a noble chapter of cricket history.

It may sound ridiculous to call a serious back injury a blessing in disguise. But it may have been just that.

Had he bowled unhindered, Dennis may have burned himself out with sheer pace. Slowing down has kept him young. It has also made him a better bowler.

The old Lillee was a little predictable. He would be fast — very fast — and the ball would swing away from the right-hander.

The slower, more recent model is full of mystery. Will the ball seam? Will it cut? Who knows? The batsman doesn't.

The wicketkeeper is a little uncertain, too, but Dennis Lillee and I have played cricket together for a long time and we have an understanding.

But if you think I'm going to let you — and every opposing batsman in the world — into the secret, then you're not as smart as I thought.

The fact that he is able to so vary his attack makes Dennis not only the best fast bowler in the world but also the most adaptable. If the wicket isn't lightning fast, it no longer worries him. He simply shortens his run and bowls his seamers and cutters.

I think it has improved his whole outlook on life.

It's been years since I heard him say an unkind word about a £"%x*&! curator or the £"%x*&! wicket he prepared.

It happened at the M.C.G. at five minutes to three on the afternoon of December 27, 1981.

Larry Gomes, a West Indies batsman who is going to break a lot of bowlers' hearts, was on 55 in the First Test of the series and giving us a lot of trouble.

Greg Chappell, at first slip, had mentioned to me a few minutes earlier that Larry was a very nice bloke but would look much better from afar. Like back in the pavilion. We say things like that on the field, you know.

So Dennis ran in, bowled . . . and Gomes got the outside edge.

You'll never know how much I wanted that edge to come my way. It was almost a psychological necessity.

Dennis had provided me with a world record by finding the edge of Ian Botham's bat only six months earlier. The least I could do was to return the compliment by snapping up Gomes.

I don't know who to blame — Dennis for finding a somewhat thick edge, Gomes for not snicking it just a little finer, or Chappell for not allowing the ball to hit his chest or something, juggling it — and letting little Rodney Marsh complete the catch.

Couldn't you see it? Greg fumbling and old Rodney throwing a glove under the ball an inch — no, a centimetre — above the ground. Catch of the year? Catch of the century? Didn't matter to me.

But I would dearly love to have been part of the dismissal — his 310th — that made Dennis Lillee the most successful Test bowler in history.

Dennis didn't give a stuff who caught that ball. For him, the ordeal was over.

His jubilation produced one of the best pieces of unrehearsed choreography the M.C.G. has seen (rivalling Sunil Gavaskar's quick funeral march from the wicket a season earlier).

The relief as he broke Lance Gibbs' world record was enormous.

One of my proudest moments – I congratulate Lillee on his Test wicket record.

If I seem to dwell on the shortcomings of the press, forgive me. But they had given Dennis a helluva time. When was he going to do it? How was he going to do it? Who was going to be his 310th Test victim? What a lot of bull!

He'd been expected to do it in the previous Test, against Pakistan. But he didn't take a wicket and if you didn't know him you'd swear he'd done it out of sheer cussedness. But, like I've said, Dennis Lillee is a straight-ahead man.

The ball that got Larry Gomes was, I'd say, about a yard and half out of my reach. Greg Chappell snapped it up and was first to reach Dennis to congratulate him. I probably set some sort of speed record (with pads on) to be second.

Sharing the occasion with Dennis and the team, right there and then, in front of an emotional M.C.G. crowd, was one of my proudest moments.

You may have gathered that I am a Dennis Lillee fan. Yeah, I'll admit to that.

Dennis and I have been through a lot of campaigns together. We've shared a lot of rooms and a lot of experiences, joyous and otherwise. I've kept wicket to every ball he's bowled in Test cricket. Throw in umpteen Sheffield Shield games and the World Series Cricket years and that's quite a partnership.

It's been a delight to be associated with this guy. It has also been an education, mainly in guts.

You can only imagine what the scoreline *might* have been at the M.C.G. that afternoon . . . Gomes, caught Marsh, bowled Lillee 55.

Still, Greg Chappell was captain. I guess he deserved a share of the action.

So who's Perfect?

ONLY A FEW PLAYERS of my era have been able to inspire in me a total sense of security.

Dennis Lillee is one. You know when Dennis has the ball there is every chance that a wicket is about to fall.

Ian Chappell was another. So is his brother Greg. When Ian was at the crease, you fully expected a big score. It was a nice, snug feeling. And the same applies to Greg.

Unfortunately, and I hate to say it, when Greg walked out to bat in the second half of the 1981-82 season, I knew he wasn't going to make runs. I hoped and prayed he would, for the team's sake as well as his own. But deep inside, I knew he wasn't going to fire.

What he did, of course, was go through the most shocking run of outs of any class batsmen of my experience.

I think there were a variety of reasons for his horror stretch, but they all boil down to one word — pressure.

Greg started the season in pretty ordinary fashion, which immediately brought pressure from the media. His glorious past deeds had made him a godlike figure to the media and if he didn't make a century every time he went to the crease, they wanted to know why. What was wrong? Christ, he only made 50! Was he sick or something?

There there was the Test captaincy. Greg had relinquished that by pulling out of the England tour, but he had a bit of a thing about the job. He wanted it back and he got it. He certainly didn't want Kim Hughes to get it.

Having been reinstated, the pressure was right on him to lead with unprecedented wisdom and astuteness. That in itself put great pressure on his batting.

I remember saying at Dennis Lillee's testimonial dinner in Brisbane that I was quite confident Greg would get a hundred in the Gabba Test against Pakistan.

I had no doubt that he would make a big score because the press had given him a hard time and I could sense that he was going to make them eat their words. A few so-called experts were suggesting he was over the hill. I was sure he was going to make them regret that.

I was only half-right about that hundred — he made 201. But to achieve it, he summoned a season's worth of concentration and effort. He admitted it later.

That innings drained him mentally and left him psychologically ill-equipped to face the rest of the summer.

It wasn't so much a matter of physical form because he's the sort of player who needs little practice. You can get him in

Greg Chappell in his horror stretch – the word was he was "over the hill".

August, after a four or five-month lay-off, and he'll be in top form again after a session at the nets.

No, it was all in the mind. He had overspent his concentration on that Brisbane innings. It was as easy as that.

It was a crying shame to see him run up that string of ducks and low scores when you knew the man was capable of such grace, elegance and brilliance.

The measure of his class had always been that he made it look so easy. You would look back on his first thirty runs of an innings and find yourself unable to remember a particular shot, unless it was a really bad ball that got the hammering it deserved.

It was the way he worked a good ball away for two or three that stamped him as a champion. Or the way he'd pick the gap with a perfectly-timed drive to the boundary. It was all so effortless.

He'd usually take 70 or 80 minutes to reach 30, simply stroking the ball around the field. Having reached that stage, he would continue to play basically the same game, but with even more finesse.

Then the truly memorable shots would come. Ah, it was pretty to watch.

I think Greg relaxed so much after that double-century in

His Majesty . . . Greg Chappell ruled against Pakistan with a double century. And this fan from his beloved 'Gabba outer proposed "the loyal toast".

Brisbane that he really didn't care. He'd shown the critics what he could do — what he could still do — and I think he talked himself into believing that the innings had automatically guaranteed him a season full of runs. I've got 200, I'm back in form, I've shown the bastards, I'll just play well from here on in.

But he didn't. A few previously-unnoticed technical flaws began to appear. Instead of playing straight down the line early in his innings, he was fending at balls he would normally have ignored.

After the first couple of ducks, you could see he was terribly anxious to get off the mark. Far too anxious. And the harder he tried to get those first runs, the worse his plight became.

Who was it said when you're hot you're hot and when you're not you're not? Greg certainly wasn't. It is a vicious circle. When your confidence is down, your form is down. And when your form continues to slip, what confidence you have left goes with it, only faster. Worse still, poor Greg was our captain.

Not until the final Test against the West Indies in Adelaide did Greg really come good. He made a very gutsy 61 in the first innings, gutsy because he batted with a broken hand.

It must have been a blessed relief for him after a summer he'll never forget. And yet that summer of failures may be the making of Greg Chappell the captain. I think it taught him that he is, after all, only human and that those around him are mere mortals too.

Greg had always been a perfectionist who could not tolerate fools. It would upset him if one of his team made a fielding error or bowled a bad ball. I think he will get less upset from now on because he knows what the world "fallible" is all about.

Everyone makes mistakes. The great players make fewer. Greg has always been one of the great players and he found it difficult to understand why all those around him were not similarly blessed.

I think the summer of 1981-82 taught him to understand. And I think he will be a better captain for it.

Burying a Monster

The MCG "killer-pitch" gets its come-uppance.

THERE WAS EVERY reason for utter gloom in the Australian dressing room at the M.C.G. on the evening of January 24, 1981. The West Indians had just walloped us again to take a 2-0 lead in the one-day finals and it was going to take some sort of miracle to save us from a whitewash.

But beneath the depression, there was a glimmer of relief: we had played on that bloody M.C.G. pitch for the last time! The bulldozers were moving in the very next day to dig up that treacherous turf. It was long overdue, but it was happening.

The happiest among us was skipper Greg Chappell, who had made it his business — perhaps his obsession — to see the death sentence passed. Greg had called that wicket a lot of things — a disgrace, an embarrassment, a potential killer — and none of us disagreed with a word he said.

In retrospect, I suppose Greg's vendetta may have been partly responsible for Australia's poor performances at the M.C.G. over the seasons of the wicket's decline. He may have unwittingly played into the opposition's hands by convincing his own men that the pitch was atrocious, unplayable and what have you.

We'd have looked less like a pack of whingers had we gone out there with a more positive attitude and let our bats do the talking. It would have made us look 100 per cent sincere. As it was, people maybe got sick of hearing us complaining after a defeat.

But that's all very well in theory. In practice, it was another thing again. The M.C.G. strip had developed into a monster, certainly unfit for first-class cricket and possibly not up to village green standard.

It had reached the stage where to win the toss at the M.C.G. was to win the game. You won the toss, you batted first and you made your runs — as many as possible — while the pitch was playing reasonably for the first couple of days. Then you stood back and watched the opposing batsmen prod, poke and get out as the pitch went from bad to worse to horrible.

The 1981 Test against the West Indies, which we won quite comfortably, was one of Australia's few good recent performances at the M.C.G. And remember, we won the toss and batted!

In my experience, Australian batsmen have always performed better when the ball has been coming on to the bat with an even bounce. We are, after all, teethed on those pitch conditions. Perhaps we are spoilt, but when you consider the huge money flowing to the Australian Cricket Board these days, I think we are entitled to the best playing conditions. We certainly do not deserve anything as crook as the M.C.G. was serving up to us.

There may be excuses in other parts of the world where the authorities simply do not have the money to inject into ground and wicket improvements. There are no excuses whatsoever in Australia.

As secretary of the Melbourne Cricket Club, Ian Johnson had long been the "father" of the M.C.G. pitch. I think that's why he was so reluctant to see radical change.

'Johnno' would always be out in the centre before the start of a big game and it was impossible to extract from him any sort of enlightening appraisal about the state of the strip. It would be "good", he would say, "just like it has been for 30 or 40 years".

I don't think he appreciated that the pitch had, in fact, changed — and changed appreciatively — over those 30 or 40 years, for the worse.

Neither was he living strictly with the times. He was still attuned to his own playing days when spin bowling played such an important part in Test cricket.

'Johnno' was entrenched in his own era and, having been a spinner himself, was unable to come to terms with the speed age. He could not, or would not, admit that an era dominated by

The MCG thoughts of Marsh – a baseball glove?

express bowlers demanded pitches which gave the batsman a fighting chance to make runs or, at very least, defend himself. You don't mind facing the fastest bowler in the world (you mightn't relish it, but you don't really mind it) provided you know that the ball is going to bounce evenly. Sure it may seam and swing all over the place, but you have a chance of surviving if the bounce is regular.

The M.C.G. pitch gave you no such chance. Rarely would two balls pitched on the same spot behave similarly. One would climb off the pitch, the next would shoot through low.

Ian Johnson has some funny ideas about cricket and he's a very stubborn man. Actually, I've always got along well with him, much to the dismay of some of my team-mates.

In 1975, I was fortunate enough to be invited, under Cathay Pacific sponsorship (must give 'em a plug) to the closing-down ceremony for the old Hong Kong cricket ground. I was the only present-day player in the party. 'Johnno' was among the many past players invited. I talked to him at length about cricket in his day and we became very friendly. Sure, he's got his airs and graces, but I reckon he's entitled to them. I've never let him get away with them, though.

No matter what the situation or circumstances, I greet him with "Goodday, 'Johnno' — how are you going, you silly old bugger?" . . . or words to that effect.

Cartoonist Tandberg's view of the Australian batsmen's plight on the treacherous MCG pitch.

We became so chummy that just before I left for the 1982 New Zealand tour, he asked me for an Australian blazer for his cricket museum. I gave him one, too, which was probably a bit of a shock to him.

But, like I said, Ian Johnson is a very stubborn man and it must have deeply hurt his pride to see his precious M.C.G. pitch dug up. Something had to be done though — and fast.

The Australian Cricket Board had threatened to wipe out the M.C.G. as a first-class cricket venue and the Victorian Cricket Association had already switched Sheffield Shield games to Geelong and St. Kilda.

John Maley, a genius with a blade of grass, but spurned by those at the top.

I think the A.C.B.'s ultimatum was the clincher as far as 'Johnno' was concerned. Not even a man as stubborn as he was going to see the world's greatest cricket ground laid to waste.

The drama should have ended with the decision to dig up the pitches, a decision that should have been made years earlier. But it didn't. The John Maley fiasco was still to come.

Maley is arguably the best cricket curator in the world. A lot of people think he's a genius, that he could produce a magnificent wicket from two sheets of corrugated iron laid end to end in a cow paddock. I don't know about that, but he was certainly the best man to oversee the resurrection of the M.C.G.

It may yet prove to be a tragedy that Maley turned down the job and caught the next flight back to Perth because the Melbourne Cricket Club would not allow him a free hand.

I'm a great believer in allowing experts to do the jobs which demand expertise. 'Johnno's' mob obviously don't see things that way. They may live to regret it.

It was always interesting — but never a pleasure — to keep on the M.C.G. pitch in its state of decline. It made you wonder how Russian roulette ever became so popular.

I always thought the situation was more suited to a baseball glove than the regulation wicketkeeper's gear. You never knew when an express delivery was going to run along the ground until it kicked up at your feet and smacked you in the face. It was a continuing nightmare.

It certainly didn't impress visiting 'keepers. Pakistan's Wasim Bari and India's Syed Kirmani made their feelings plain to me during their recent tours. So did David Murray when he kept for the West Indies in 1981-82.

These guys would generally come into our rooms for a drink after a day's play and you could see the relief on their faces. They'd survived to fight another day.

"Thank goodness that's over", they'd say. "How do you do it all the time?"

The answer was that you did it with a lot of luck. You were lucky to be alive and you were lucky if you didn't let a Bradman score of byes through.

You think back and you wonder how good Richie Robinson might have been had the M.C.G. not been his home ground. The poor bugger had to play four Shield games a season there! Go back through the Sheffield Shield records and you'll notice that Richie rarely figured in a bagful of dismissals. That is simply because the ball has the dastardly habit of keeping low at the M.C.G. so you do not get a lot of catches standing back.

Just ask Kirmani about the ball keeping low. During the M.C.G. Test of the last Indian tour, he copped a fiendish delivery from Kapil Dev. A dead-set grubber. It rocketed along the ground, then reared up at him and nearly took his head off. The ball lifted him into the air as it cracked him in the shoulder and one of the blokes in the dressing-room remarked that it looked like a rabbit being shot with a Remington bullet. Kirmani was lucky to survive.

Ask anyone who played on that M.C.G. pitch before its long-overdue demise and see if you can find a kind word for it.

Greg Chappell deplored it. Desmond Haynes said it was a disgrace. Clive Lloyd, the world's most experienced professional cricketer, said it was a disgrace. The umpires said it was a disgrace. Some of our blokes were frightened to play on it.

For one of the one-day games against the West Indies, the wicket was prepared wet. I don't blame anyone for saying he was frightened to play on it — not when Michael Holding was bowling at something like 100 m.p.h. and making the ball do incredible things. You'd have been safer facing a firing squad.

The shame of it all has been that the state of the pitch has seriously damaged the M.C.G.'s reputation as a great cricket ground. Certainly, it has an atmosphere that no other ground in the world can produce. Its standing depends on what is achieved before the start of the 1982-83 season.

We await the resumption of play with breathless anticipation.

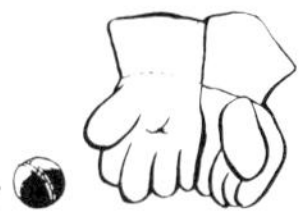

King for a Day

ASK ME WHAT it feels like to captain Australia and I've got to admit that I really don't know. I'd done it several times — while Greg Chappell or Kim Hughes were off the field for an over or two attending to personal needs (yes, we have bladders and bowels, you know) — but the experiences were too brief to leave me with any lasting impressions.

Then, when my big chance came (two full innings of the Adelaide Test against the West Indies early in 1982), the only sensation I felt at the end of each day was exhaustion. Sheer physical and mental exhaustion. I guess that's the result of greatness being thrust upon you.

It was quite a Test match for me, that Adelaide game. It was my 80th, which broke Neil Harvey's record of appearances for Australia. The statisticians would find something significant in that little landmark.

We lost the match, which gives me a 100 per cent failure rate as skipper for any length of time. But it's no real disgrace to be beaten by the Windies, and we drew the series anyway.

Captaincy is something that appeals to any cricketer who's been around a while and I am no exception. Why should I be?

Why, indeed, should a wicketkeeper not captain Australia or any side? Who but the wicketkeeper knows more, apart from the bowler and the batsman, about how the wicket is playing, what it is doing? The 'keeper lives, after all in the batsman's pocket. He quickly learns his strengths and weaknesses, how to get him out (or at least unsettle him).

Of course, the slips fieldsmen are pretty handily placed for that sort of stuff, too. And because Greg Chappell is and Kim Hughes is sometimes brilliant in the slips cordon, Rodney Marsh wasn't exactly holding his breath as he awaited his country's call.

The events leading up to my emergency captaincy of Australia in Adelaide were quite dramatic and, for once, largely unknown by the press.

A lot of flak had been fired by the newspapers, leading up to that Test, about Greg Chappell's woeful run of outs with the bat. They came up with 'Chappello' (as distinct from 'Chappelli' — Jesus, they're clever, aren't they?) and filled a lot of heads with the idea that Greg would be sacked as skipper for the New Zealand tour. They also said that Kim Hughes had personality and communication problems and wasn't keen on the captaincy anyway and that I, by the process of elimination, would lead the team to New Zealand.

Unless you were close to the situation, you could not even

John Dyson earned a beer, but not the headlines.

imagine the pressure Greg was under in that batting horror stretch. His past deeds had elevated him to superhuman status in the eyes of the press — and didn't they enjoy bringing him down! They took to illogical conclusions the old bit about the bigger they are the harder they fall.

The affair reached farcical proportions in our second innings of the Sydney Test against the West Indies. Greg made a duck; John Dyson hit up a magnificent, unbeaten 127 to save the game.

And who got the headlines? Greg Chappell.

What about Dyson? Since when did a duck outweigh a century? It was a diabolical piece of newspaper work.

Sure, we didn't like Greg failing either, but we knew the best way for him to regain form was for the rest of us to lift our games and take the pressure off him.

For too long, Greg had been the mainstay of our batting. If he didn't get runs, Australia didn't get runs. It was an unreal strain to put on one man. Any man.

Greg cracked under that pressure after the second one-day final against the Windies in Melbourne. He'd been dismissed yet again for a low score and he was completely shattered.

He came off the field, walked downstairs where I was putting the togs on, came straight up to me and said: "Well, that's it, pal."

He shook my hand and said: "Thanks for all the good times we've had together during our careers. I'm officially retired."

Jesus, I thought, this can't be right. We're only halfway through the one-day finals. We've got the last Test match to go. There's no way known he's going to pull out.

I didn't say much at all. I just said: "Are you serious?"

"Yes," he said.

I thought I'd best let it go at that for the moment. He'd just got out. Maybe he'd cool down a little later. So later that afternoon I followed him into the showers (hey, don't get any funny ideas about either of us!). I showered alongside him and said: "Hey listen, mate, are you serious about that or not?"

He assured me that he was.

I said: "Well, I don't really agree with you, but is there anything we can do to change your mind?"

"No, my mind is made up," he said. "I'll be informing Phil Ridings (Australian Cricket Board chairman) and that's that!"

He said the same sort of thing that day to several of the other guys.

Well, the West Indies thrashed us and the scene was set, as we sat in the dressing-room having a beer after the game, for a bit of aggro to emerge. And it sure did.

Kim Hughes did the press conference that night and said our

fast bowlers weren't as quick as the Windies', weren't as young, and the Australian selectors would have to unearth a couple of quickies — and pronto — even if it meant scouring the beaches.

For Chrissake, what sort of a comment was that! It certainly wasn't one of Kim's great moments in diplomacy.

Dennis Lillee heard about it (the reporter who was helping him write his column for the Sydney *Sun* was at the conference) and was nice and angry. Dennis and Kim don't often see eye to eye and they had quite a verbal blue.

A few other things were being said that night, too. Certain players said things about the ability or otherwise of other players. It was typical of a team who'd just been soundly beaten twice in a row.

I don't believe this is a bad thing. Better to talk it out there and then than to think about it, brood over it and mumble it behind someone's back. At least you know where you stand. You've had your say, you've got it off your chest, now let's get back together and play cricket.

The bickering went on for quite a while. We had a few more drinks and carried it from the M.C.G. back over the road to the Melbourne Hilton, into the team room. We continued our discussions, over a few more beers, and the subject of captaincy inevitably reared its head. I don't know why it had taken so long. Maybe we just didn't know how many of us knew.

So Greg Chappell was going to quit. It was out in the open now and the best-laid plan of Rodney Marsh was implemented . . .

"Look," I told them, "I don't care if he does retire. It's fine by me. I'll take over!"

That shook them more than a little.

"Gee," they said, "hadn't thought of that. We thought Kim would be next in line."

"Maybe he is," said I, "but we won't let him do it. I'll do it!"

It was a bit outrageous of me because Kim was there at the time. But he agreed.

He said: "I think you're the man for the job. I think you're most qualified to lead us."

About half a dozen of the other guys agreed. It was very flattering.

My cunning little mind told me that Part 1 of the plan had been an unqualified success.

Part 2 was to go upstairs and wake Greg Chappell . . .

Greg was sleeping a little uneasily and didn't take much waking. I sat on the end of his bed and explained the process by which I was going to take over the captaincy of the Australian cricket team.

Kim Hughes would have maybe another year or two, I said, to give him a bit of breathing space and let him irremovably entrench himself as a Test batsman.

So that left Greg — who'd quit — and yours truly. I asked him what he thought about that.

Greg said he had no ambitions left.

"That's probably why I'm not playing well," he said. "I find it very hard to motivate myself to go out and get runs day after day.

"I feel as though if I don't get runs, the team don't get runs and I just can't continually play under that sort of pressure.

"I thought I'd got over it when I made the 201 against the Pakis in Brisbane. But I had to work like hell. I thought that might be the turning point, but it really wasn't."

He was starting to sound as if he'd never come to the bit I'd mapped out for him in my devious little mind.

But then he said it:

"I guess if I've got one ambition left, it's to captain Australia against England next year and get back the Ashes."

Bingo!

That's precisely what I wanted to hear. Rodney Marsh — master psychologist — had pulled it off.

Greg Chappell is a very smart bloke, but Rodney Marsh had conned him!

By merely suggesting that I was happy to captain Australia, I'd raised his hackles. You could see them rising under his pyjamas. At least I think they were hackles.

Greg came downstairs and we had a long and meaningful team discussion. The skipper was back in his rightful place.

Phil Ridings phoned him next morning and Greg agreed to captain the side for the rest of the one-day finals and in the Adelaide Test. That's another thing the newspapers never got to hear about.

As the press stumbled about in the dark, the rumours persisted that Greg would get the khyber and that I would be named skipper for the New Zealand tour.

So the A.C.B. did a damn wise thing by coming out on the eve of the Adelaide Test with an official assurance that Greg would be captain if he was selected for the Kiwi trip — in other words, if he *wanted* to go.

It was an unprecedented move by the Board and, in the circumstances, the best thing that could have happened. It took a lot of pressure off Greg and, consequently, off the rest of the team.

I thought he played extremely well in that Adelaide Test. We were 3/8 when he went in and his painstaking 61 — along with Allan Border's 78 — held the innings together when all looked lost. It was great to see Greg relax a little. He knew the guys were behind him; he knew none of us wanted him to retire.

So what happens? Greg breaks his finger, Kim Hughes (playing with a broken toe) is crippled by a blow to the instep — and Rodney Marsh, who'd been making noises about captaining Australia, suddenly is.

And to make life more miserable, Dennis Lillee breaks down after only a few overs in the first innings and deserts me for the first time in his life.

But injuries aside, it was a mighty proud moment for me to lead Australia. Even the gentlemen of the press gave me a pass mark.

As I said, I learned the true meaning of the word "exhaustion" but I'll never forget the way the guys pitched in and fought like hell on my behalf. I'm very, very grateful.

We lost the Test but, all things considered, did ourselves or Australia no disservice.

We were 4/17 after about an hour on the first day and it was after 6.00 p.m. on the fifth and final day before the "invincible" Windies were able to wrap it up. Given ordinary luck with injuries, we'd have saved the match. Maybe we'd have won it.

Then again, a fit Greg Chappell and a fit Kim Hughes would have deprived Rodney Marsh of several hours of near-glory . . .

More play, more Pay

MUCH HAS BEEN written and said about the structure of the present-day Australian cricket season and its effects.

Is there too much cricket? More specifically, is there too much one-day cricket? Are the Test matches coming at the right time? Are the fans deserting Tests for one-day cricket?

There is no doubt that one-day cricket has caught on in a big way because it is the cricket of our times. The average cricket fan today is younger than his predecessors and this is the type of game — instant cricket — which appeals most to him. It will continue to attract young folk, to the detriment, unfortunately, of Test match crowds.

Personally, I much prefer Tests to the one-day affairs, but I'm prepared to live with the changing times. Anyone who fights progress is a fool. If the future calls for more one-day matches, then you'll hear no objections from Rodney Marsh.

I'm not particularly enthusiastic about the idea because I find this instant cricket mentally and physically exhausting and I prefer the sustained drama of a five-day Test. But I'm a professional cricketer and the more cricket I play the fatter is my pay cheque. Those among us who refuse to see things that way obviously have more money than logic.

We, the players, are as much responsible as the administrators for the structure of our season. We have a players' committee — a sub-committee of the A.C.B. — which has a say in the programming. Theoretically, every first-class player in Australia has a vote for his representative on the sub-committee and that representative is supposed to report back to the players of each State squad to tell them exactly what's going on and to seek their opinions.

I say theoretically because it hasn't worked that way in Western Australia nor, I believe, in any other State.

Still, if the players have a complaint about the season's programme, it's up to them to make a noise about it.

Too much cricket? Not as far as I'm concerned. Not while there's a quid involved.

Sometimes it hurts – but the pay cheque eases the pain!

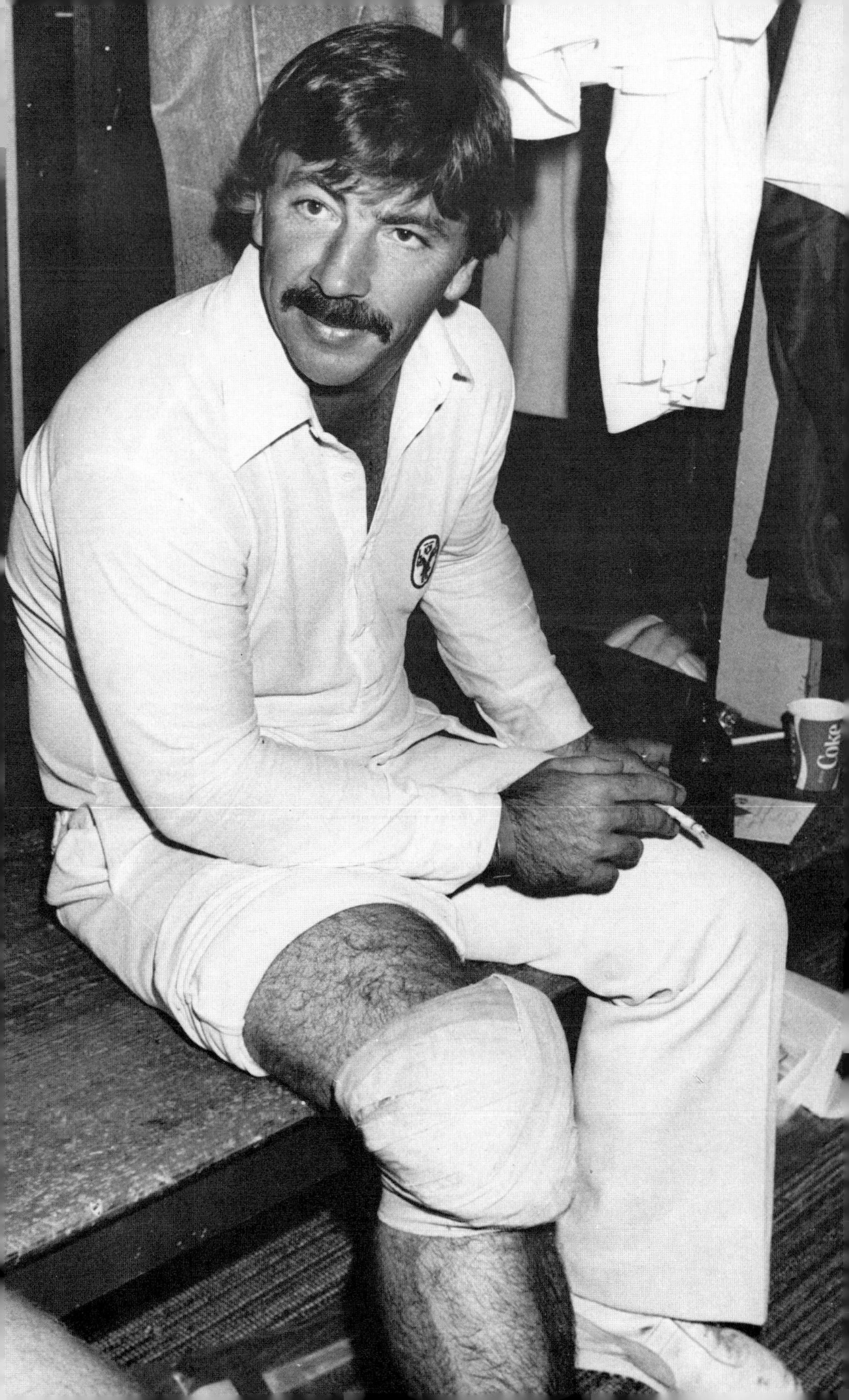
Coke

My devastating Dozen

INEVITABLY AND OFTEN, in casual conversation or in clinical questioning, I am asked to name the best composite Australian cricket team of my experience.

The answer does not come easily because there are variables, notably the strength of the opposition from one season to another.

I have selected the players who, in my opionion, have performed best against the strongest opposition thrown at us.

My team is:

1. Bill Lawry
2. Bruce Laird
3. Ian Chappell (captain)
4. Greg Chappell (vice-captain)
5. Allan Border
6. Doug Walters
7. Rodney Marsh
8. Ashley Mallett
9. Graham McKenzie
10. Dennis Lillee
11. Jeff Thomson
12. Ian Redpath (12th man)

A lot of people will read my name in this list and accuse me of egotism. But the whole point of the exercise is to choose the best I have played with. The rules of selection therefore assure my spot in the line-up.

Bill Lawry is my first choice as opening batsman despite my limited experience of him. I played only five Tests with 'The Phantom' and I was pretty young at the time. But here was a man with a tremendous record, a fearless approach to fast bowling and the ability to be a fine stroke-maker when the mood took him.

Bill's defence was immaculate; he was basically a front-foot player, which gives him a bit of an edge over other Australian openers of my time.

Most opening bats of today, particularly Australians, tend to play off the back foot, but Bill used his height and reach to great advantage. He was able to get on to the front foot to the well-pitched delivery and force it away on either side of the wicket, not always for four, but very often for runs. And if it got him away from the strike, so much the better as far as he was concerned. I think Bill got great delight in occupying the crease for a long time, even if a lot of it was spent at the bowler's end.

Ross Edwards, my former West Australian and Australian

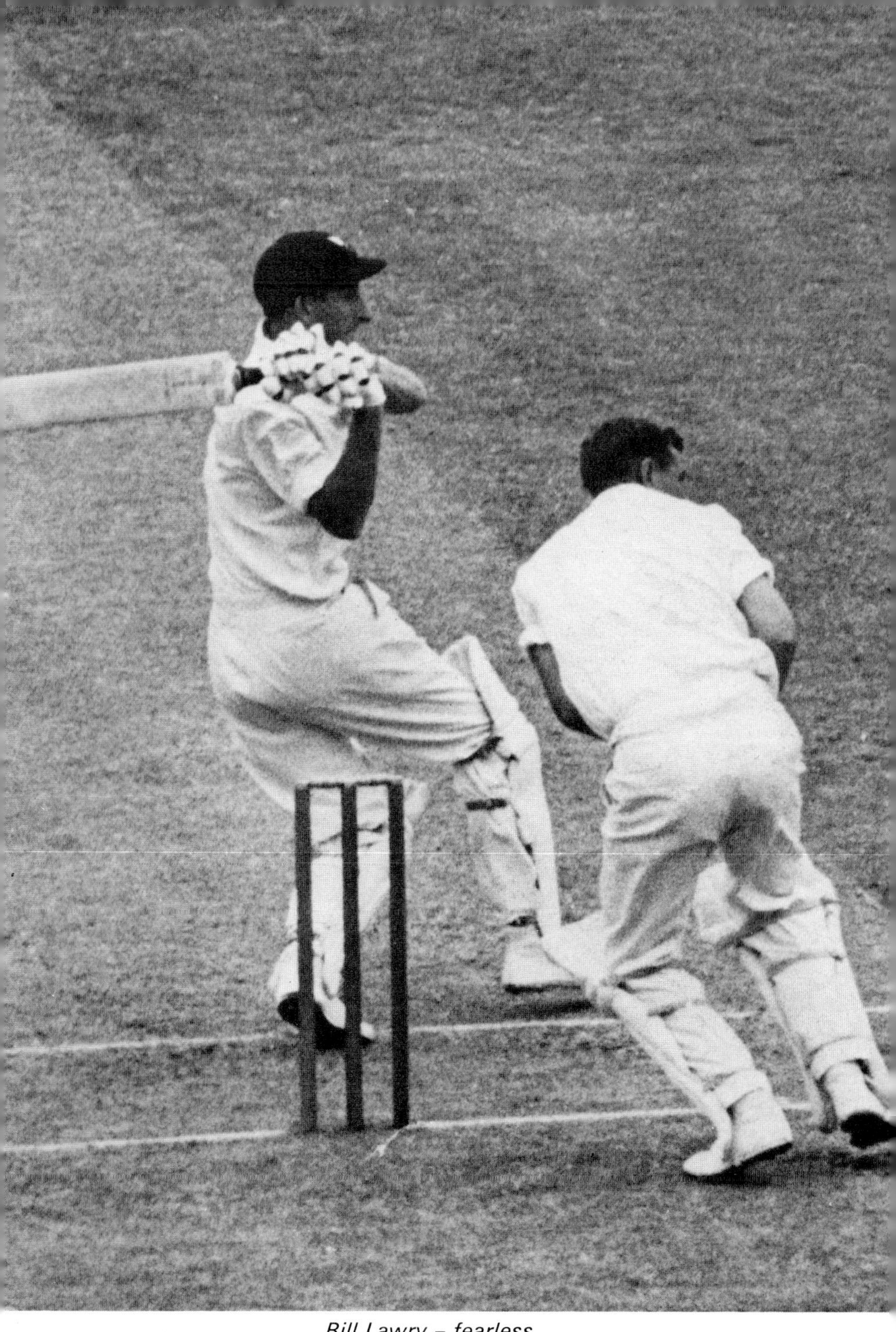

Bill Lawry – fearless.

ERG

(Above) *Graeme Wood – headstrong.*

(Left) *Bruce Laird – rated by West Indies.*

team-mate had the same philosophy. He figured that if you weren't on strike, the only way they could get you out was to run you out. And who — apart from a few yahoos in the outer — gave a damn if you took your time getting your runs?

Being a left-hander made Bill all the more difficult for the pace bowlers to handle. They would have to adapt to him, and that very often meant loose deliveries and easy runs. Bill had the ideal temperament for an opening batsman, was a good tactician and a very safe fieldsman.

Team him up with Bruce Laird and you have the opening combination to frustrate and infuriate the best pace attack imaginable.

My selection of Bruce may surprise a lot of people, but I regard him as the best player of quick bowling I have seen. I know the West Indians rate him very highly.

Bruce is predominantly a back-foot player, which would make him the perfect foil for Bill Lawry. He is a fine batting technician, very correct and very quick between wickets.

Having batted so often, in Shield and Test matches with Graeme Wood, I'm sure Bruce would relish the cooler head and judgement of Lawry in taking the quick singles. There is a vast difference between "quick" and "suicidal".

A Lawry-Laird combination is not the sort of partnership from which you would expect a flying start. You could not, nor would not, compare the natural flair of these two for hitting the ball with that of, say, West Indians Gordon Greenidge and Desmond Haynes.

But flying starts are not what I'd be looking for. Maybe for the one-day matches, but we're talking about Test cricket. The real thing.

Lawry and Laird together would provide undeniable solidarity, the foundation on which to consistently build a big score (bearing in mind the quality of the batting to follow). And isn't "solid" what opening partnerships should be all about?

There is a time-honoured theory that opening batsmen are supposed to take the shine — not the cover — off the ball. Bill and Bruce would do just that. It is a pity they were not contemporaries.

It was tempting to put Ian Redpath into one of the opening berths. 'Redders' was a great stroke-player when conditions were favourable and a real fighter when they were not. He was also a terrific team man. But in the context of a team to perform best against the best possible opposition, he loses out against Lawry and Laird because marginally he was less of a batting technician.

Keith Stackpole also looms large. 'Stacky' was a real goer. He was so attacking that he thought defence was something you built around de house!

But he was technically ill-equipped to handle a sustained, all-pace attack. 'Stacky' would have taken the attack to them and sometimes — just sometimes — he would have beaten them. It would have been stirring, red-blooded stuff, but not percentage cricket. And percentage cricket is the thing opening batsmen must play.

A four-pronged pace attack — such as the West Indies have been able to maintain for so long — would have worked 'Stacky' out fairly quickly and got his measure. He was great entertainment value and he made a lot of runs. But as a long-term proposition against a pace attack with both quality and quantity, I prefer others.

Graeme Wood is another class opener. He rules himself out of my team at this stage because of a few shortcomings which have nothing to do with his batting ability. Graeme tends to regard a Test match as being a one-innings affair. He seems to think that a score in the first innings exempts him from making runs in the second. I'm sure he is overcoming this fault. I'm sure that the more experience he gets on wickets outside Australia the more complete an opening batsman he will become.

He is already a stylist, a nice blend of aggression and correct technique. When he learns to stem that rush of blood to the head — and he will — he will be a cricketer to behold. Perhaps if I'd written this chapter two or three years hence, Graeme would have been the first man I'd selected. For the sake of Australian cricket, I hope it turns out that way.

Suppose, then, both openers are, as they say, back in the pavilion. We now have the brothers Chappell in tandem.

We'll deal first with Ian, the best captain I've played under, so, obviously, skipper of my elite team.

It is fascinating to envisage what Ian's Test batting average might have been, batting at No. 3, if he'd come in after what could be regarded as an average start to the innings.

Unfortunately, worthwhile opening stands were a rarity in his career, so more often than not he went in to face the new ball. Worse than that, he had to face an attack geed up by the capture of an early wicket. In retrospect, I suppose this turned him into a more complete batsman, but one wonders what he might have done if the pressure had not been so intense and so consistent. Ian was a fine defensive player when the situation so demanded. Attack, however, was his natural game. 'Chappelli' in full cry was a glorious sight and his strokes covered all parts of the ground.

And let me say a few words — surprising words, perhaps — about his bowling. Ian bowled very little at first-class level, but I regard him as the best leg-spinner to whom I've kept wicket. I've always maintained he should have used himself more. The only thing lacking in his bowling was accuracy and you can put that down to lack of practice and experience. But as a technician of the gentle art of leg-spin, he was tops in my book.

Had he not been captain, he might have been called upon to do more bowling — and I think Australia's success rate would have been all the better for it. Perhaps he was modest, although that doesn't sound like the Ian Chappell I know so well.

Ian was a born leader, a man who led by example. No player was asked to do anything Ian himself couldn't do.

His captaincy theory was to let the game run its natural course as far as possible. Yet if anything had to be tried, if a punt had to be taken, he was prepared to do it sooner than any other captain I've served. In many cases, I thought he'd made a bowling change sooner than was warranted. But he would prove me wrong almost immediately by making a break-through with the tactic.

Admittedly, he had a lot of talent at his disposal during his captaincy years. Australia were on top of the heap — but good as we were, he made us better. I think his handling of the Test sides

Ian Chappell – born to lead.

Greg Chappell – inspires confidence.

of his era made us look better than we actually were.

He could be undisputed boss and one of the boys at the same time. He was magnificent in fostering team spirit and ever ready to help youngsters and develop their attitudes towards the game of cricket.

As a competitor, he was fierce and unrelenting. He gave the opposition nothing. Opponents may not have particularly liked Ian Chappell, but they damn sure respected him.

At No. 4 in my team of "all-stars", who else but Greg Chappell?

Just as brother Ian would have thrived on coming to the crease when a little of the shine was off the ball, so Greg is tailormade for No. 4 rather than first drop. Unfortunately, until the 1981-82 season, he found himself far too often in virtually opening the innings.

There is no doubting Greg's champion qualities. A magnificent batsman, a more-than-useful medium-pace bowler and the best fieldsman I have seen, whether in slips or in the outfield.

When Greg Chappell strides to the wicket you get that feeling that Australia are in safe hands. Ian inspired the same confidence.

Interestingly, Greg and Ian were rarely associated in big Test partnerships. Maybe, having grown up together, they knew each other too well. Certainly, each batted better when the other was not at the other end.

If there is a criticism to be made of Greg's batting, it is his performance against spin on a turning wicket. He struggles a little in these situations because his style is so correct that he finds it hard to adapt.

I'll always remember Ian telling me that when the wicket is turning, the batsman must improvise. Pull the ball to leg from wide of the off-stump . . . that sort of thing . . . break up the field and create your own gaps. Ian did that very well; Greg lacks his older brother's inventiveness, his flair for producing the unexpected.

But who's to criticise the talents of Greg Chappell? Not Rodney Marsh. Greg Chappell is a magnificent all-round cricketer.

While the brothers Chappell were automatic selections at No. 3 and 4 in my team, there were quite a few candidates for the next two berths. Ian Redpath was one of them. So was Ross Edwards. So was Kim Hughes.

I settled for Allan Border and Doug Walters, in that batting order.

I've played Test cricket with Allan Border only since 1979 — but in that time he has averaged better than 50. We've played together in Australia, New Zealand, Pakistan and England and

Allan Border – adapts.

I've marvelled at his ability to adapt to any type of wicket.

The West Indies pace attack had him guessing for a while, but he has intense powers of concentration and he simply put his head down and learned how to cope with non-stop speed.

Physically, he is a very strong little bloke and a ferocious hitter of the ball when ferocious hitting is called for. He is also a first-rate fieldsman and a very handy change bowler. Ideally, I would bat him at No. 6, but that spot is already reserved for the best No. 6 I've seen — Dougie Walters. I prefer Allan down the order because of his ability to bat with the tail, to protect the low-order from the strike and to attack or defend as fortunes fluctuate. He's held us together many times and I see him going on to become one of Australia's all-time great batsmen.

All-time greats? Doug Walters is already a member of that club.

I realise that hindsight counts for nothing, but I still maintain Doug's omission from the 1981 tour of England may well have cost us the Ashes. He had topped the averages during the 1980-81 Australian summer, and though his record in England wasn't brilliant, I think his experience would have pulled us through those two amazing cliff-hanger Tests which we lost. I think we could have counted on him averaging, say, 30 in the Tests. As it turned out, that would have been enough to swing the Ashes our way. It's pure conjecture now, but I can't help wondering.

Doug was often criticised for his unorthodox technique, but there's an old saying in golf which applies very nicely to his batting: "It's not how, it's how many!" Ian Botham gave new dimensions to that expression during the 1981 series.

Doug was an ideal No. 6 because although he was so often left protecting the tailenders, his scoring rate rarely varied. You could count on him to score his first 50 in about 100 minutes and, if he went on to a century, you could bet it would come up in about 200 minutes.

If the captain was looking at a possible declaration, Doug was a delight because you could just about set your watch by him. You could set your run target, do a little simple, projected arithmetic — and Doug would do the rest. He was a tremendous player of spin and a savage puller of the ball — two attributes which further enhanced his suitability to the No. 6 spot.

The bowlers were often pretty tired by the time Doug sauntered to the crease and there was none better than he to take full advantage of their fatigue. Sure, he had a couple of lean years, but I think the emergence of the batsman's helmet put him on the road back.

Doug was vulnerable against sustained pace and made no secret of his dislike of the bouncer. But, really, who among us relishes the bouncer? Who wants a broken head? I'm not suggesting that Doug was frightened of the short-pitched stuff. I'm just saying he preferred it not to happen. He felt a lot more secure batting in a protective helmet and that confidence was reflected in his performances. Maybe he should still be playing Test cricket.

Doug Walters – all-time great.

Yours truly – a matter of numbers.

Doug was an extraordinary team man, a real humourist who was largely responsible for keeping the team so close-knit in the golden years of the early 1970s. He was also an uncanny partnership-breaker with his medium-pace bowling — his 49 Test wickets speak for themselves — and the best cover fieldsman, from a run-out viewpoint, of my time.

A lot of people might consider Paul Sheahan or Ross Edwards better exponents of cover-fielding, but give me Doug Walters any old time. His ability to pick up the ball on the run and hit the stumps with it — and in the one action — sets him apart from any other. Not bad for a bloke who always thought the word "training" had to do with travelling by rail.

No. 7? Well, it has to be me because, as I said earlier, we are confining this team to my era and nobody else has kept wickets for Australia in that time. I shan't go into the details of what a helluva bloke I am.

Before we start on the bowlers it's worth noting that we already have four very handy part-timers in the team — the Chappells, Allan Border and Doug Walters. None in the all-rounder class of Gary Sobers or Ian Botham, but handy nevertheless.

I've chosen four bowlers, but I'll leave it to a more experienced captain than I to slot them into batting order.

For the sake of argument (and it may start a few) I'll put Ashley Mallett in at No. 8.

I never regarded 'Rowdy' as a master batsman, although he made some very useful Test scores. I doubt if his eyesight, which was less than 20-20, would have done much for long-term survival against the West Indies pace barrages we saw in the 1981-82 series. I think most of his runs would have come from the outside edge.

But I'm looking at Ashley as the finest spin bowler I've played with or against. He gets my nod for this ahead of "new boy" Bruce Yardley and "old boy" John Gleeson.

'Rowdy' loved a challenge. The better the batsman at the other end, the better he bowled. Such was his temperament. He was built just the right way for an off-spinner. Tall. His height allowed him to easily vary his pace and trajectory, which is the hallmark of a great exponent of his particular trade.

'Rowdy' had a very fine arm ball, bowled one that went straight on and when the wicket was turning, he spun the ball alarmingly. His control was immaculate and I can fault his bowling on only one count: He tended to "buy" his wickets against the tailenders. He would give the ball more air when the lesser batsmen were at the crease and concede unnecessary runs in the process. 'Roo' Yardley has the same failing.

Having bowled tightly and splendidly against the recognised batsmen, 'Rowdy' would throw the ball too far up, enticing the tailenders into "suicidal" big hits instead of letting the wickets come by nagging away on a good length. Sometimes it worked; sometimes he got a caning before it worked; sometimes it didn't work at all.

Apart from being an extraordinary off-spinner, 'Rowdy' was the best gully fieldsman we may ever see. In the 1974-75 series, when we regained the Ashes, some of his catches in that position were unbelievable. Even more so when you consider his poor vision. Gully is perhaps the most difficult of all catching

(Above) *Graham McKenzie – amazing physique.*

(Left) *Ashley Mallett – made it look easy.*

positions. Slips is tough enough, but the catches there come from the edge of the bat — and there are three or four blokes to juggle the responsibility and the ball. But in the gully, you're all on your own, mate — and the stroke is usually the full-blooded square-cut. I'd demand danger money to field at gully. Ashley made it look so easy. He'd merely thrust out a hand and the ball

would stick as if glued. I'll let you into a secret here. Ashley comes from a baseballing family — his brother Nick represented Australia — and 'Rowdy' himself was a catcher in the game.

I remember going to the night baseball at the W.A.C.A Ground as a youngster. My mates and I would stand behind the catcher's plate (protected by the wire mesh, of course) and heap all kinds of abuse on 'Rowdy'. Sometimes I wonder if he's ever forgiven me.

There are three fast bowlers in my team and as much as I respect the ferocity of the West Indies' four-pronged attack, I think my trio would more than even the score.

Dennis Lillee is obviously my first choice. And if you think I'm going to reach for more superlatives — even if he is a close mate — you're wrong. If I say any more about him in this book I'll be tempted to charge him for advertising space.

My second choice is Graham McKenzie. I leave myself open to criticism here because I didn't play a lot of Test cricket with 'Garth'. And even then he was what a lot of people might call "past his prime". But the word "prime" never really applied to Graham. He was always a "prime" fast bowler, as feared and respected at the end of his career as he was several years earlier.

An amazing sportsman. No-one ever thought of him as an express-pace bowler. No-one that is, except those who faced him. He had a very short, almost leisurely, run-up and he generated extreme pace by pounding the ball into the wicket with those magnificent shoulders of his. No wonder they called him 'Garth'. His physique and strength were the source of many gags. Someone once said he could hold a bull out to wee-wee. I never doubted it.

'Garth' could change pace without giving the batsman — or the wicketkeeper — a flicker of an indication of what was happening. He would send down a few very quick ones, then whip in the blistering ball-tearer with no apparent change of action. He would merely bend the back a little more — and you had to be standing behind him to see that. The pace of that extra-quick delivery would almost knock the wicketkeeper off his feet. Spare a thought (if you're generous) for the batsman!

The crying shame of it all is that Graham had to carry the Australian pace attack for a decade. His value as a strike bowler therefore became somewhat lost in his invaluable role as a stock bowler.

In the end he was second only to Richie Benaud as Australia's greatest-ever Test wicket-keeper, until, of course, Lillee came along to rocket past them all. Imagine what McKenzie would

Dennis Lillee – world's best.

have done with real support — a Lindwall or a Miller, a Lillee or a Thomson — operating from the other end. Devastating, I'd say. He'd have bowled shorter spells, he'd have been fresher, more lethal. Maybe Dennis Lillee would still be chasing 'Garth's' record!

Imagine too, what a lighter workload might have done to his batting. Graham wielded a better-than-average willow for a bowler but you couldn't blame him for devoting not too much attention to run-making, particularly towards the end of his career. He'd done enough. He would have developed into a better all-rounder in my team.

Jeff Thomson — unpredictable, terrifying 'Thommo' — is the third member of my opening attack. I think I'd start the action with Lillee and McKenzie because Jeff has very often been most damaging when a little of the gloss has been taken from the cherry.

Jeff has had more ups and downs than a Myer lift-driver, but he's still as dangerous — and as quick, in short spells — as any bowler in the world.

Michael Holding, the forefront of the West Indies battery, can sustain top pace over a longer spell, but Jeff, at his peak, is as quick and perhaps a little more shocking. By that I mean that he still produces more unplayable balls than anyone else, on a pro rata basis.

He had a horrid Test debut, against Pakistan in 1972-73. Mind you, if you were a fast bowler with a broken toe, you mightn't have set the world afire either.

But some of my fondest — and most painful memories — in cricket are shared by Jeff Thomson.

I took a few catches as he ran through England in 1974-75 and the West Indies in 1975-76. It was an incredible experience standing back (well back) behind the stumps as 'Thommo' ran in to bowl. Maybe it was the breeze flapping their trousers, but I could have sworn I saw a few batsmen's knees shaking.

'Thommo' then was all pace and little discretion. He'd bowl one wide down the off-side; the next one would be wide down the leg-side; the next would be spot-on! Made it interesting for me.

The balls I took hurt like hell but it was a pleasant kind of pain. Thud! Ouch! At least you'd see the ball. The batsman hadn't.

Jeff's slingshot action produced his unreal pace and unprecedented bounce from a good length. It also put intolerable strain on his right arm and shoulder . . . hence his injury problem.

Jeff Thomson – dangerous.

Ian Redpath – a real fighter.

He is still a magnificent bowler, wiser now and prepared to bowl a batsman out rather than blast him into submission. At his peak he was a one-man invasion. He is still a man to strike fear into the heart — and perhaps the bowels — of the enemy.

Every great cricket team needs a Jeff Thomson.

But don't take my word for it. Just face him yourself in the nets one day.

Slipterisms

AMONG HIS OTHER achievements, on and off the field, Lennie Pascoe invented the Slipterism. It has nothing to do with the Spoonerism, fade mamous, I believe, by the Rwo Tonnies, Carker and Borbett.

No, the Slipterism is altogether different. It is the gem of phrase which only Lennie can produce and is derived from his nicknames, 'Slippie' or 'Slipter'. I'd love to tell you how he acquired those nicknames, but it is something best left to his inevitable autobiography, which will be very well worth reading.

The Slipterism comes in many shapes and sizes but is invariably uttered in dead seriousness. That's what makes it so funny.

A few examples of this art form:

* On the 1977 tour of England, we ran across Geoff Boycott in a lead-up game to the First Test. Jeff Thomson was the most feared weapon in our armoury on that tour and, wisely, captain Greg Chappell didn't want to fully expose 'Thommo's' wares before the main event.
  So his specific instruction was: "No bouncers to Boycott!" 'Thommo', though, has always been a creature of habit and promptly let Boycott have a couple of short ones.
  Greg was furious and made his feelings quite plain.
  "Oh well," said Lennie, with wisdom beyond his years, "Ya can't expect a leopard to change its stripes!"
* After one international match of the 1981-82 season, manager John Edwards asked the Australian players if they'd mind coming to him individually to pick up their cheques.
  Lennie looked him straight in the eye and said: "Wouldn't it be better if we came one at a time?"
* We were sitting around in the dressing-room at Bath (no anti-Pom jokes, now) during the game against Somerset in 1977 autographing the interminable cricket bats. We'd already signed a heap of them before I noticed that Lennie had written his name upside-down.
  "You bloody dummy," I said, "you've signed your name the wrong way up!"
  "How did you know it was me?" he asked, straight faced as you like.
* The Pascoe pride and devotion to cricket is such that even if he's physically exhausted after a long bowling spell, he'll beg another over.
  Bowling is his go and I reckon if they changed the laws, he'd

operate all day, alternating end-to-end.

Greg Chappell found him hard to dislodge from a bowling spell that memorable day Dennis Lillee took his Benaud-breaking 249th Test wicket.

It was pretty hot at the M.C.G. and Lennie had already sent down a long spell. "Righto, mate, that's enough," said Greg.

"Just one more over . . . just one more," pleaded Lennie.

"No," said Greg.

"Oh go on, Greg, just one more," Lennie implored. "I've only got 230 to break the record!"

* Lennie had a pretty patchy 1981-82 summer. It took him a good deal longer than he'd expected to regain match fitness after his knee surgery and was out of the Australian team more often than he was in it.

During one injury-enforced lay-off, he bobbed up at the nets in Sydney to practice with us. He rightly figured it would help us out and improve his own fitness at the same time.

He told us that being an unemployed professional cricketer was not much fun and that he'd been forced to join the real workforce. He had sought — and had actually found — a job in the freight department with Ansett Airlines.

Team manager Edwards read about it in the evening paper and when Lennie appeared at the nets a couple of days later, said: "I saw in the paper that you've got a new job, Len. How's it going?"

To which Lennie replied: "Well you obviously didn't read the last edition, John, because I've quit!"

Yes, he'd lasted just one day.

It's surprising really because he could be an enormous asset to an airline. He's strong enough to lift a Jumbo jet while they dust its belly!

Quite a character is Lennie Pascoe. He's the type of bloke as valuable to a cricket team off the field as he is in the heat of battle because his humour does so much for morale.

I've met a lot of hilarious people since I first played cricket, but Lennie Pascoe is probably top of my wit parade.

A matter of Conscience?

ASK ME IF I'D like to play cricket in South Africa and the answer would be "yes". Ask me if I actually *would*, in the existing political climate, and I'd have to back off and do a lot of thinking, a lot of soul-searching.

I'd like to play in South Africa because I've never been there. I know a lot of cricketers who have and they tell me it's a great country to tour. But there are so many problems, so many cross-currents to consider.

I have always been dead against mixing sport and politics. The very word "sport" suggests it should have nothing to do with the political arena, but the situation in South Africa is such that a mixture of the two has long been an unfortunate fact of life.

As a sportsman, my first consideration in accepting or rejecting an invitation to tour South Africa would be the effect it might have on other sportsmen playing any sort of sport elsewhere in the world.

When this chapter was written, the full consequences of the South African tour by Geoff Boycott and his "Dirty Dozen" had still not been felt, politically or otherwise. But if the end result were to be a breakdown in international cricketing relations — a situation from which every professional cricketer in the world would severely suffer — then Boycott and his "rebels" should have trouble sleeping nights.

I'm not suggesting there will be such a breakdown. Nor do I claim to be an authority on South African politics. But I know that my conscience would say "no" to a South African tour if I thought my participation might be detrimental to any other sportsman anywhere.

The worst that could arise, I suppose, from the vexed South African question is a complete polarisation of international cricket — that is, white nations playing white, black nations playing black. I doubt it will ever come to that. I certainly hope it doesn't.

My understanding is that South Africa has done all it can to integrate its domestic cricket, to the point of satisfying International Cricket Conference demands. Yet it has still not been readmitted to the I.C.C.

The financial temptation of accepting an invitation to play in South Africa would obviously be great. Telephone-number figures have been mentioned (theoretically) for an Australian side to tour, but perhaps morals and ethics must overrule money if it came to such a conflict.

And quite a conflict it would be. If it were a question of setting yourself and your family up for life financially but endangering

Back row (l to r): *Wayne Larkins, Bob Woolmer, 'Tiger' Lance* (manager), *Les Taylor, Chris Old, Mike Hendrick, Peter Willey, John Lever. Front: Geoff Humpage, Derek Underwood, Geoff Boycott, Graham Gooch* (c.), *Peter Cooke* (organiser), *Dennis Amiss, Alan Knott.*

the future of international cricket, what would you do? What would I do? I really can't answer it because the question has been purely hypothetical.

I do believe very strongly that those of us who have reaped cricket's financial rewards should leave something other than ruins for those who come after us.

Like I've said, the question of South Africa at this stage is purely hypothetical. The easiest thing would be for it to stay that way.

The formation of the "Dirty Dozen" has been widely compared with Kerry Packer's World Series Cricket venture. I go along with that in only one respect — that both operations were planned amid much secrecy and cloak-and-dagger stuff. The comparison ends there.

The big difference is that the players who signed with Packer did so in the genuine belief it would benefit cricket and the lot of professional cricketers throughout the world. I see no such far reaching benefits flowing from the "Dirty Dozen" experiment if, in fact, such a noble cause was among their motives.

One of the things which made me smile a little inwardly was the attitude of some of the younger members of the Australian team when they heard that telephone number offers were in the wind.

Now don't forget that some of these chaps were absolutely horrified at the "defections" to World Series Cricket in 1977. They questioned our motives, among other things.

So, it came as something of a surprise to hear some of them say that if they were made big offers they would have little hesitation in accepting them. One prominent player even went into print on that one. They'd played for Australia, they said. Been there . . . and done their bit for flag and country, and now it was time to feather the nest, if given the opportunity.

How times and attitudes change.

It makes me wonder how immoral we World Series cricketers were after all!

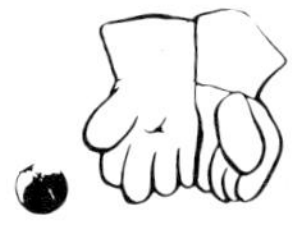

The Kiwi Caper

. . . and Greg Chappell made them eat feathers!

IF EVER I FELT like giving an overseas tour a miss it was the trip to New Zealand in 1982. And I think the other 12 players felt the same way. New Zealand sounded about as attractive to us as Ethiopia. Come to think of it, Ethiopia may have been more appealing. At least it would have been different.

It had been a long, crowded summer for us and, quite frankly, I'd had a gutful of cricket. We'd played two Test series, against Pakistan and the West Indies, a lot of one-day internationals, Shield matches and McDonald's Cup games.

We left for New Zealand only six days after the third and final West Indies Test and some of us had played a McDonald's Cup game in the meantime.

We were a pretty jaded lot.

Also playing on our minds, I guess, was the prospect of an unnerving reception when we crossed the Tasman. There had been all sorts of reports of what the Kiwi crowds might have in store for us to square up for the underarm episode in Melbourne a year earlier. If you believed some of the rumours, you'd have sworn we were going to make that Springboks rugby tour look like a Methodist picnic.

Our itinerary called for three Tests, three one-day internationals and various other excuses for cricket matches and if we'd expected the worst from the crowds, we were agreeably surprised by the mood at the first one-day game at Auckland's Eden Park.

It was a big, boisterous crowd — 43,000 of them — but we had no real whinge about their behaviour. We copped plenty of flak, but we expected it.

What annoyed us was the crowd control — or lack of it. Of those 43,000, two or three thousand were on the playing arena at most stages of the game. If it had happened in Melbourne, the police would have had a field day. There wouldn't have been enough Black Marias to go around.

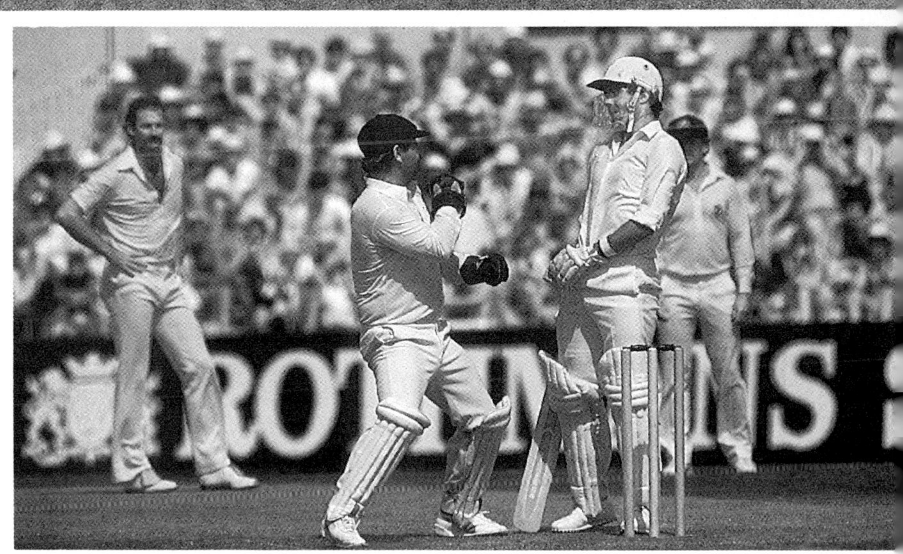

Me, hard at work . . . and at play!

All things considered, though, the reception at Eden Park was better than we'd expected. When New Zealand won, though, you'd have sworn they'd just taken Gallipoli single-handed.

The crowd left me alone because I think most of them were aware of my feelings about the underarm incident. I didn't approve. I never will.

Greg Chappell was the obvious target and they gave him little peace. Greg responded in the best possible way — by making a century. It was a great innings played in very trying circumstances and it couldn't have happened at a better time.

In the eyes of most New Zealand cricket fans, Greg was no longer that %*!!£&$% who ordered that underarm delivery. He was Greg Chappell, master batsman. His 108 removed any heat that may have been left in what had been a most unfortunate chapter of cricket history.

The Eden Park crowd had done their homework pretty thoroughly and it wasn't until a few days later that we learned the significance of one of the many banners decorating the fence. It read: "Bring on Unkovitch!"

Unkovitch? Who the hell was Unkovitch?

It was suggested that they may have been having some sort of illiterate go at Lennie Pascoe, but we read the truth in one of the newspapers.

The banner referred to Vince Unkovitch, New Zealand's lawn bowls champion.

Now there's a man who can *really* bowl underarm . . .

Despite Greg's century — an obvious return to form after what had been a harrowing season for him personally — we lost that Eden Park game by 46 runs. It was a most discouraging start to the tour but our cause wasn't helped at all by New Zealand opener Bruce Edgar being bowled when he was five and going on to make 79.

As a wicketkeeper, I've had a close-up of some amazing umpiring decisions at many levels of cricket and this ranks high among them. The umpires said they hadn't actually seen the ball hit Edgar's stumps — and neither was prepared to exercise commonsense by giving him out.

Quite obviously Edgar hadn't trodden on his stumps and quite obviously the bail hadn't blown off because there was no wind. So how did the bail get to be lying there on the ground? Easy — the ball had knocked it off the top of the stumps.

I'd started to appeal for a catch behind when I heard what I thought was a snick. I stifled the appeal when I realised Edgar hadn't hit the ball. The sound I'd heard was the ball clipping the bail. There was not a shadow of doubt that Alderman had bowled him. There could have been no other way.

I made a discreet inquiry to the umpires, who said, well, they couldn't really give a batsman out when they hadn't seen the ball hit the stumps.

I'll guarantee a lot of umpires have been in a similar position but have raised the finger because there was no logical alternative. The only other possible explanation for that tell-tale bail being on the ground is that one of our fieldsman had powers of levitation and willed the bloody thing off the top of the stumps.

Edgar didn't walk, as most batsmen do when they're bowled, because he didn't know for sure. I don't blame him. Neither did I blame Greg Chappell for standing his ground when Martin Snedden claimed he had "caught" him at the M.C.G. during the celebrated underarm match.

I'm one of the few people who still believes Greg was not out that day. The television replays showed Snedden taking the ball, sure enough. But who's to say that the ball — even a small part of it — did not touch the ground as he took it?

It's amazing how different sets of standards are applied to different players. Greg was canned for "poor sportsmanship" after that so-called catch. No-one — certainly no-one in New Zealand — accused Edgar of anything similar after the Eden Park bail incident.

Later that day, as I awaited my turn to bat, I discussed the Edgar "dismissal" with "Dicky" Bird, that doyen of English umpires, who was an interested spectator at the game. I asked him how he would have reacted had he not actually seen the ball hit stump or bail.

"Well," he said, "I'd have used my commonsense and given him out because there was no other possible way of the bail getting on to the ground."

"Dicky" Bird's word is good enough for me.

The Edgar decision was the first of many "shockers" which were to go against us on that tour. As far as New Zealand umpiring goes, our education had barely begun.

The second example of how not to umpire a game of cricket reared its head with the first ball of the third and last one-day international.

It was bowled by Jeff Thomson to John Wright and it was nothing more than a warm-up ball which pitched on leg stump and would have missed the off.

Wright could and should have let it go — but you don't do that sort of thing in one-day cricket. He played at it, got a very distinct edge and if Terry Alderman did not possess such fine reflexes, the ball would have gone between first and second slips. As it was, Terry snapped up a magnificent catch, fully 18 inches from the ground. It was as clear-cut a dismissal as you could imagine.

Only if the ball had sent the three stumps cartwheeling out of the ground could you have been more thoroughly convinced. Yet as we ran our various ways to congratulate Terry and 'Thommo', Wright stood there as if frozen. I'd seen a lot of blokes refuse to walk, but this was ridiculous!

A few of the boys started muttering things like "Eh, come on, he's out" and "What's going on here?"

Wright eventually turned and walked — but at no stage did the umpire actually give him out!

The papers next morning quoted the umpire's explanation: NO-ONE HAD APPEALED! No-one had appealed so he couldn't give a decision! What sort of logic was that? Maybe they play different rules in New Zealand.

The fascinating thing was that one of the papers carried a picture of John Wright being caught by Terry Alderman — with Jeff Thomson, arms outstretched, appealing vigorously. Perhaps we'd misread the tourist brochures. Perhaps you have to lodge an appeal in writing.

On this occasion, we had merely said to ourselves and each other: "You beauty. He's out. Caught." How stupid of us not to have formed an orderly queue, approached the umpire individually, bowed low and asked: "Mr. Umpire, how is that?"

The umpiring controversy came to a head in the Second Test in Auckland, just where it had started.

We'd already had our fill of Kiwi umpires. We'd appealed ourselves hoarse in the First Test for very little result. We'd learned that it was impossible to be given out LBW if you got on to your front foot. It didn't matter if you played a real shot at the ball or not. The local umpires had taken the front-foot theory to its illogical conclusion.

What we didn't know — because we hadn't yet seen enough of the umpiring — was if the rule applied to both sides or if it changed innings by innings, as the umpires saw fit.

The umpires empanelled for the Second Test were no strangers to us — Steven Woodward, who'd made the extraordinary non-decision on the Wright catch, and Bruce Bricknell, who was at square-leg when Alderman bowled Edgar in the first one-dayer.

The Test started very poorly for Australia. We were all out in our first innings for 210 and the run-outs of Chappell and Allan Border certainly didn't help our cause.

New Zealand replied with 387, but we figured we only needed 178 to win because we'd already bowled them out twice. I say that with tongue in cheek but really, I've never experienced a day like March 14, 1982. I have never seen so many appeals — genuine, confident appeals — turned down. We were accused later of appealing frivolously, in desperation, giving a shout for almost anything. That's rubbish.

If our appeals became desperate it was merely because we were knocking up seeing them turned down. It was the rawest umpiring deal I've seen handed out to any team, anywhere in the world. I thought we did very well to keep our cool. A lesser team may have taken things into their own hands and walked off. It wouldn't have done us any good, of course, except to perhaps relieve a lot of frustration.

I could never condone West Indies fast bowler Colin Croft's physical clash with umpire Fred Goodall during the Second Test at Christchurch in 1980. It is unforgivable to abuse or assault an umpire or referee in any sport. But as I watched appeal after appeal stoically turned down on March 14, Croft's misdeed became easier to understand.

We didn't expect to get the nod every time we shouted, but I lost count that day of the number of decisions — unanimous appeals for what we considered were clear-cut dismissals — which went against us. At one stage, I decided I'd like nothing better than to take off my gloves, lay them neatly on the ground, say "I hereby retire from this game" — and walk off. I didn't, of course, but the temptation was great.

I've always had a fairly well-developed sense of fair play and I'm not suggesting the umpires were not fair. I'm not even suggesting that they were excessively patriotic. I'm just saying they were completely incompetent. And in the end, they were too frightened to make a decision.

Funnily enough, two decisions Bricknell gave against New Zealand were very, very wrong. He said Geoff Howarth was run out when he obviously wasn't. And Ian Smith, the wicketkeeper, wasn't even close to being leg-before when he was given out for it. Bruce Yardley, the bowler at the time, didn't even appeal for the Smith decision. I did — and I did it alone — because I thought if they weren't going to raise the finger when a bloke was obviously out, maybe they would when he obviously wasn't. It was some sort of lunatic reverse psychology brought on by chronic frustration.

It worked, anyway.

I don't like appealing when I'm satisfied a batsman is not out. But when umpires make so many mistakes, you've got to clutch at straws — or anything else that floats by.

When stumps were (mercifully) drawn that day, the New Zealand players came into our room for a drink and they were visibly upset and embarrassed by what had happened out there on the field. I think their embarrassment outweighed our anger.

At the tea adjournment, our boys had sat there and, instead of fuming, they'd laughed. They actually sat there and laughed. That's what we thought of the umpiring. It was a bloody joke. A bad joke, but a joke just the same.

In retrospect, I'm glad we accepted it that way. The events of that day could have developed into a most unpleasant incident. Greg Chappell deserves great credit for keeping his players calm and for remaining calm himself.

I'd spoken with West Indies players about their turbulent 1980 tour of New Zealand and they made plain their opinions of the umpiring. They had a lot of trouble, particularly with LBW decisions, and I'm sure the Colin Croft-Fred Goodall incident was born of sheer frustration.

Like ourselves, the Windies had just played an Australian season and I guess they'd had enough. The fatigue, the business of living out of a suitcase probably did nothing for their dispositions and only accentuated their displeasure with sub-standard umpiring decisions.

Clearly, something must be done to lift the standard of umpiring, not only in New Zealand, but everywhere.

How often does a Test series go by these days without some sort of complaint or controversy about umpiring? Tourists come to Australia and criticise our umpires; we go to India or Pakistan and complain about theirs.

Perhaps the time has come for the cricketing nations to get together and come up with a panel of umpires — the best in the world — to officiate here, there and everywhere.

I don't think neutral umpires are the answer because it's not so much a question of neutrality as it is of competence.

And I cannot see the standard improving in Australia until umpiring becomes a full-time job and not merely a sideline.

Quite a lark at Pukekura Park

THEY COULDN'T ACCUSE us of having been a dour bunch of win-at-all-cost tourists in New Zealand. Not after our one-day romp against Central Districts at New Plymouth, they couldn't.

We had not exactly relished this fixture because it had been jammed into an already-crowded itinerary. We finished a game against the President's XI in Christchurch at 5.00 p.m. on the Monday — a game which had attracted a crowd of about 600 over the three days. If Doug Walters had been there, he would be able to give you the exact crowd figure because he had a habit of counting heads during his idle moments on the field.

Anyway, it was up at 5.30 a.m. to catch a 7.00 a.m. flight to Wellington and then a Fokker Friendship (no breakfast provided) for the flight to New Plymouth, arrive there 10.15 a.m. for a scheduled 11.30 start. We barely had time to get our bags into our rooms and grab a bite of breakfast.

We were less than amused. We were tired, hungry and a little stroppy. And being in that mood we decided that the game should not be taken too seriously. Kim Hughes was captain for the day (Greg Chappell had shrewdly given it a miss and gone straight on to Auckland) and he was more than happy to go along with a little light-hearted stuff. Actually, I think it was his suggestion.

Whenever such a frivolous mood overtakes a cricket team, all sorts of fancy ideas are put forward. I, for example, had never opened the bowling for Australia and to be given the new ball before Dennis Lillee appealed to me as an enormous coup. Kim agreed.

It was then pointed out that no-one in memory had opened both the bowling and batting in a recognised one-day match. O.K., so I would face the first ball, too. This was my big chance to make my name as a phenomenal all-rounder!

We batted first and my career as an opening batsman turned out to be an unqualified flop. I was bowled for a duck by a fine off-cutter from a young bloke named Jamieson.

Still, there was my bowling to come. This would obviously be an outstanding success, but it was also bound to produce a big problem. I mean, how was I to open the bowling and keep wickets at the same time in all my future Test matches? Never mind, we would consider that later.

What seriousness there was left in our approach to this

particular game of cricket became somewhat lost in the magnificent surroundings in which it was played.

Pukekura Park is possibly the most beautiful cricket ground in the world. It is cut out of the side of a hill and looks rather like a natural amphitheatre. A magnificent place to play cricket and soak up the sun that was shining so brightly that day.

Those batsmen not actually at the wicket could be seen strolling through the beautiful gardens feeding the ducks rather than keeping an eye on the state of the game and assessing the capabilities of the attack. It was a most relaxing stroll through the gardens and I think the crowd got the message that our desire to win was less than 100 per cent ferocious.

Allan Border got right into the casual spirit of the thing by coming in at No. 3, after my dismissal in the second over, and playing some of the most diabolical, agricultural slogs I've ever seen on a cricket field. Then having found himself unable to hit every ball out of the ground, he decided to play cricket. He put together a very fine 76.

Kim Hughes came in at No. 4 wearing an Australian tie with his regulation cricket gear. He'd announced his intention of doing so in the bar the previous night. The press boys bet him $50 that he wouldn't. Kim accepted and we spent the winnings in the hotel at New Plymouth after the game.

Alan Crompton, our manager, wasn't at all amused by Kim's dress. Neither was he impressed with Graeme Wood batting at No. 11 when we were five down for not many.

At this stage, Alan approached 12th man Jeff Thomson, who was wearing T-shirt, bermuda shorts, sandals, a floppy white hat and sunglasses. Would Jeff mind, he asked, changing into respectable cricket gear, going out there and returning with Kim's tie?

Jeff convinced Alan it would be a helluva bind to change out of his civvies because he was enjoying the sun so much. Couldn't our physiotherapist, Derek Adler, do it?

As vice-captain that day, I thought it time I stepped in. I could see Alan's point. He feared we might be accused of making a mockery of the New Plymouth fixture. I could see Kim's point, too. And the team's point.

Had we been consulted about the New Zealand itinerary before we left Australia, we would certainly had queried the wisdom of the New Plymouth game. We had all been through a pretty hectic season in Australia and the last thing we needed was a helter-skelter tour of New Zealand, stopping off here, there and everywhere to do our stuff before crowds Dougie Walters could have comfortably counted individually in the first few overs.

That tie – comment by Mitchell.

My idea of the ideal itinerary would have been three Tests and three one-day internationals.

It would certainly have been a more profitable programme for the New Zealand Cricket Council. It would have shortened the tour by two weeks and saved our hosts a lot of money. They lost financially on most of the minor games and then there was the considerable cost of accommodation, fares and the like just to keep us in the country.

Perhaps Kim overdid the picnic approach by batting in his tie. Perhaps his point would have been taken had he worn the tie to the wicket and taken it off after facing a couple of balls. As it was, he'd been batting in it for about 20 minutes when I walked out to the wicket to retrieve it.

"Captain," I said, "I have a message from the manager. The message goes as follows: You are to take off your tie!"

"Tell him to go and get stuffed," Kim replied.

"I'll go back and tell him that if you like," I said.

Kim thought better of it, took off the tie and passed it to me saying a few uncomplimentary things in the process about the Australian Cricket Board for having us play this game.

The removal of that tie had the effect of ending our unofficial team "protest". We had buggered around long enough and we decided it would be a good idea to win the game.

Unfortunately, we had let things go a little too far.

My immediate personal ambition was to rewrite a few records in my opening spell of bowling. I didn't. My figures were 0/18 off 3.5 overs.

They should have been better than that because I had one bloke plum LBW but the umpire wasn't interested. I'm not kidding, it was one of the most outrageous decisions I've seen. It was surely the most outrageous decision of my somewhat limited bowling career.

We lost that match, and the crowd of about 4000 left picturesque Pukekura Park delighted with the day's play in general and the result in particular.

We should have won. The locals were nine down, 11 runs short and the last bloke in couldn't bat at all.

But cricket can be cruel. The winning run — from the second-last ball — was a gentle nudge to Lennie Pascoe, standing a couple of yards from the bat. It was the simplest run-out imaginable — and Lennie misfielded.

Off my bowling, too!

I'd had a big day.

I decided to stick to keeping wickets.

A man called 'Piggy'

ALL OF US WHO had been through the underarm incident had wanted to meet New Zealand Prime Minister Robert Muldoon, the man they call 'Piggy'. We wanted to see for ourselves what sort of a man would call us cowards.

It was Muldoon, you'll remember, who made an international incident of the grubber which ended the one-day match against New Zealand in Melbourne on February 2, 1981.

I think my feelings about the underarm ball are fairly well-known. I didn't approve. Neither did I approve of Muldoon's outburst. He called it an act of cowardice and found it "most appropriate" that the Australian team had been dressed in yellow. He also called it the most disgusting effort he could recall in the history of cricket — "a game which used to be played by gentlemen".

We'd talked a good deal about this 'Piggy' guy and he probably wouldn't have got our vote if he'd called a snap election.

We met him, unexpectedly, in Wellington in February, 1982, during our New Zealand tour. The occasion was a cocktail party thrown by the Australian High Commissioner. We had no idea that Muldoon would be there, but up he bobbed, large as life. He was introduced to us by team manager Alan Crompton and I'm delighted to report that the boys didn't let Australia down.

Dennis Lillee set the ball rolling. He apologised to Muldoon for not wearing his yellow shirt. He felt sure Muldoon thought we should all be wearing yellow shirts, being the cowards that we were.

'Piggy' didn't offer a shot at this one. He merely smiled and let the matter rest.

Then Allan Border and Graeme Wood took up the attack. Allan raised the subject of the caricature of Muldoon in Larry Pickering's classic calendar. Have you seen it? he asked.

"Yes, I have," said Muldoon — and Allan asked him what he thought of it.

The answer was couched in typically-political generalities, but Graeme Wood wanted something more specific.

"Is it really true that you've got a band-aid on your left ball?" he asked.

Again, 'Piggy' merely smiled . . . and walked away.

Greg Chappell, who had more reason than any of us for wanting to meet Muldoon, was in particularly fine form at the High Commissioner's function. Seeing the ball particularly well, you might say.

In a private chat with the Prime Minister, Greg also apologised for not wearing his yellow shirt and Muldoon said not to worry, that he'd come along to one of our one-day games to see us in our true colours.

Muldoon said he had a fervent interest in cricket (which surprised Greg) and that only the previous weekend, he played in a match which he had organised. Incredibly the match ended in a tie, each side scoring 431.

In a speech to the gathering, Greg again apologised for the absence of yellow shirts. He then referred to Muldoon's tied cricket match.

"Only a politician", said Greg, "could have organised something like that."

When Greg made reference to another tie — the New Zealand election — it nearly brought the High Commissioner's house down.

He also said that he'd just heard from Malcolm Fraser who felt that in view of the extremely good finish to the tour, the lot of us should go to Sinai to help out with the peace-keeping force.